BEAUTY FOR ASHES!

A COLORING BOOK FOR INSPIRATION AND REVELATION

BEAUTY FOR ASHES
A Coloring Book for Inspiration and Revelation

Published in the United States by When Heaven Speaks, LLC
P.O. Box 55
Pooler, GA 31322
www.whenheavenspeakspublishing.com

Copyright © 2020 TWYLIA G. REID
ISBN: 9798578675874

All rights reserved. No part of this book may be reproduced, distributed, or transmitted in any form by any means, graphic, electronic, or mechanical, including photocopy, recording, taping, or by any information storage or retrieval system, without permission in writing from the publisher, except in the case of reprints in the context of reviews, quotes, or references.

Unless otherwise indicated, scripture quotations are from the Holy Bible, New International Version (NIV).

Special discounts are available on bulk quantity purchases by book clubs, associations, and special interest groups. For details, email: info@twyliareid.com or call 912-335-3799.

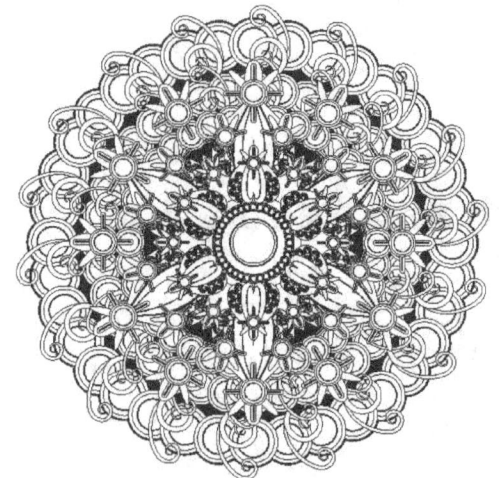 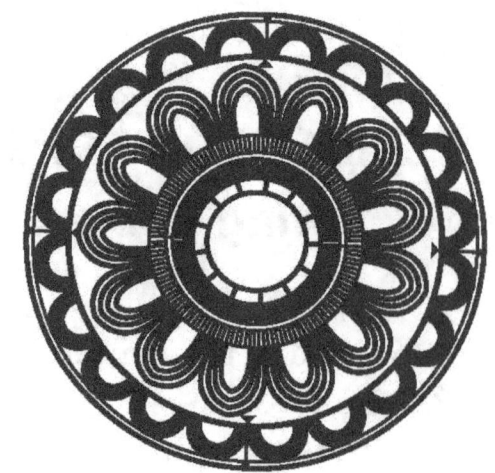

This Book Belongs To:

....

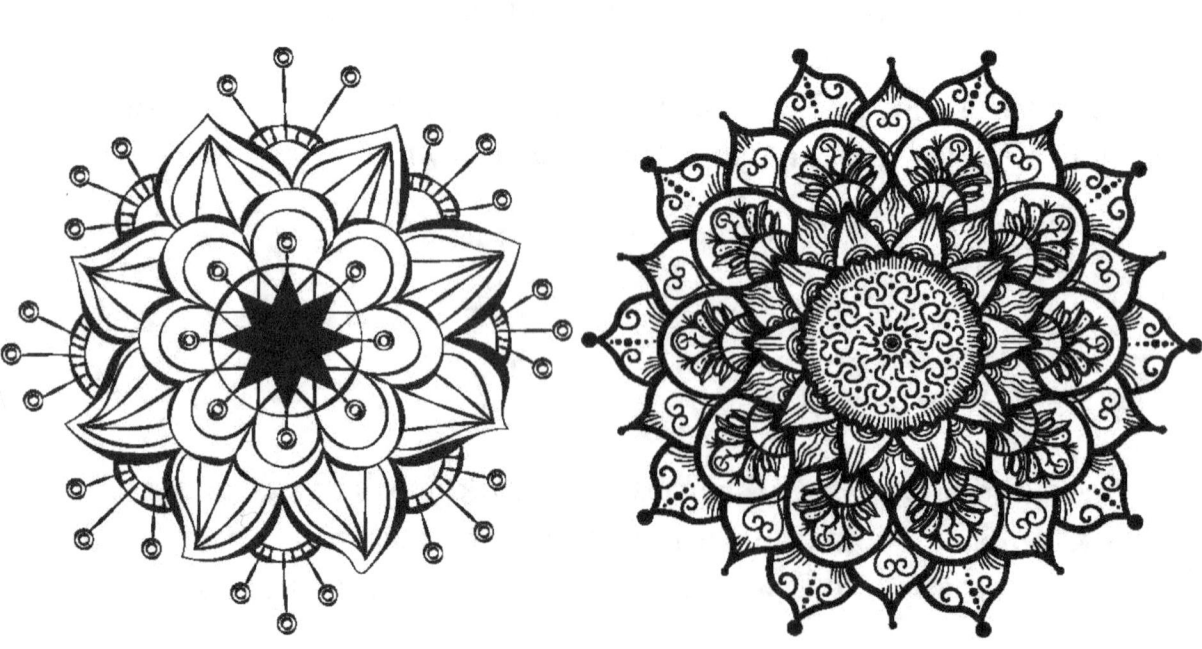

BEAUTY FOR ASHES

Life is beautiful! It's truly what you make of it! We display photos and beautiful images all over social media. We share amazing stories with our family and friends that paint the perfect picture in spite of what we may be really feeling deep inside.

No one sees the true struggle you may be dealing with deep down inside that may cause the most unbearable pain ever. When the entire world all around us is filled with wars and rumors of wars, injustices, and even a pandemic it can become difficult to see the true beauty God gives us each day. Isn't it beautiful that God says He can give you beauty for ashes? We love that. I think we concentrate on the beauty, but unless you give Him your ashes, you don't get the beauty. There is a substitution plan here.

Often times this task seems impossible, but one thing that is for sure is that God is able to do all things…if we only believe! You must remember we serve a God who is not bothered by the things that trouble this earth. We serve a God who promises to bestow on us a crown of beauty instead of ashes! (Isaiah 61:3) Our God is a God who redeems and delivers. But, due to the brokenness and heartache, this world offers this can be hard to remember.

Ashes are the wounded parts of our lives. Everybody has wounds; everybody has ashes All kinds of them! Sometimes they happen with a family member, a mate, your children, your job, or even your church. Sometimes it hurts. Sometimes it's hard. Sometimes it's dark. And it leaves its mark in the deepest parts of our souls, where no one but God can really see. Ashes happen in every place. My hope is that for you, as you color within the pages and meditate on the written words, you are reminded of all the beauty God gives us each day and that God is always here with us each day.

BEAUTY FOR ASHES is about finding beauty in the small, mundane everyday areas of your life. May the content of this coloring book remind you that God is great and able to do exceedingly and abundantly above all we can ever ask or think. And, most importantly serve as a constant reminder that God bestows on you a crown of beauty instead of ashes, the oil of joy instead of mourning, and a garment of praise instead of a spirit of despair!

There are beauty and greatness behind every mark of darkness. The ashes will fall away, they don't stay forever! But, His greatness and glory shine forever through every broken place and flaw we've struggled through. I encourage those who are facing deep battles to remember God is greater than any enemy we face in this life. We overcome because He has overcome and our lives are hidden in Christ.

May God cover you with His peace, may He bring healing in the face of adversity, may He bring deep, abiding joy when nothing else makes sense, and may He bring comfort and care as He wraps you in His loving arms.

So, as you color and glean upon the finished pages, I pray it will be a constant reminder that although this world is broken, our Lord and Savior is not!

He has made everything beautiful in its time.

He will come to us like winter rains.

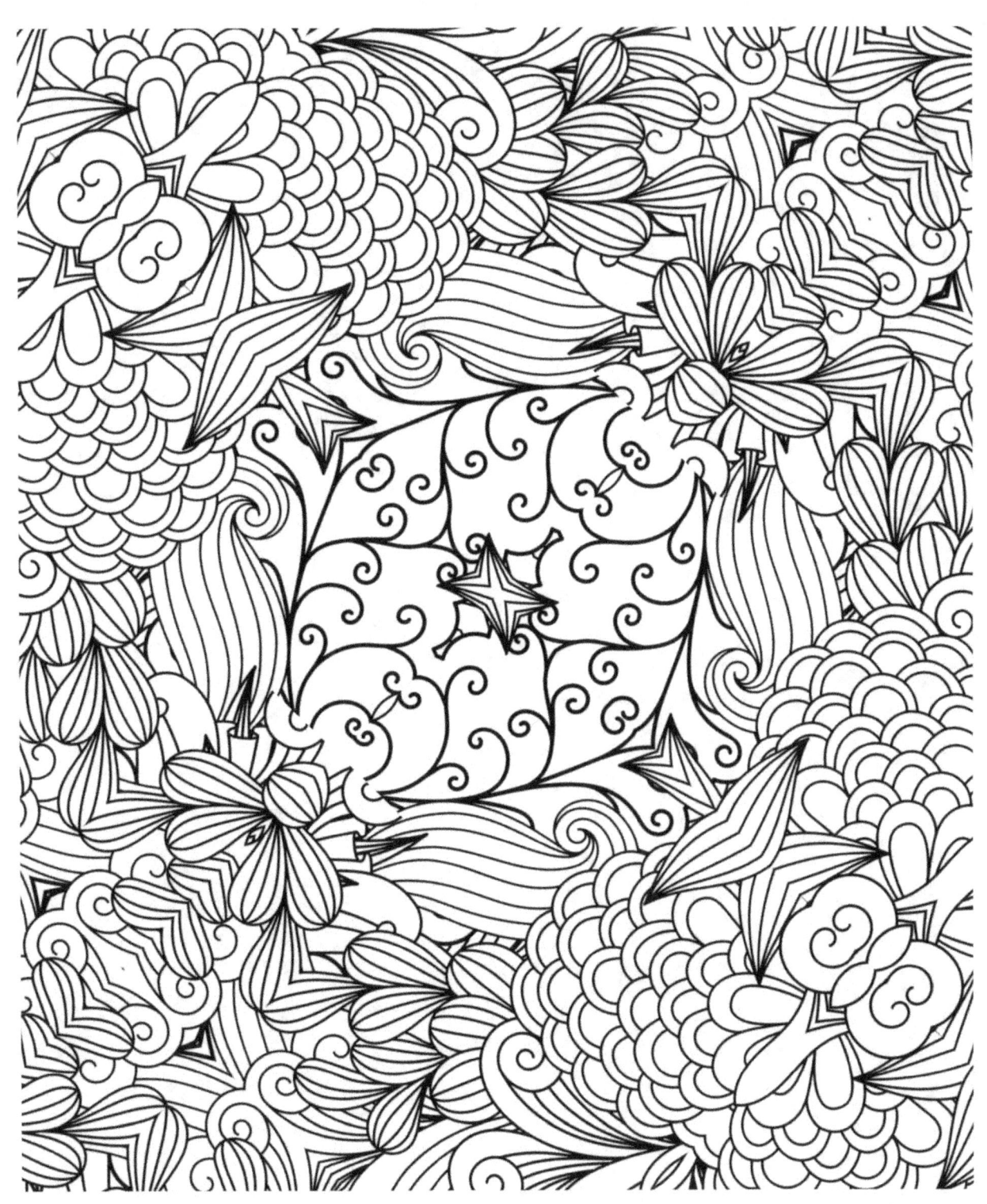

Rejoicing comes in the morning.

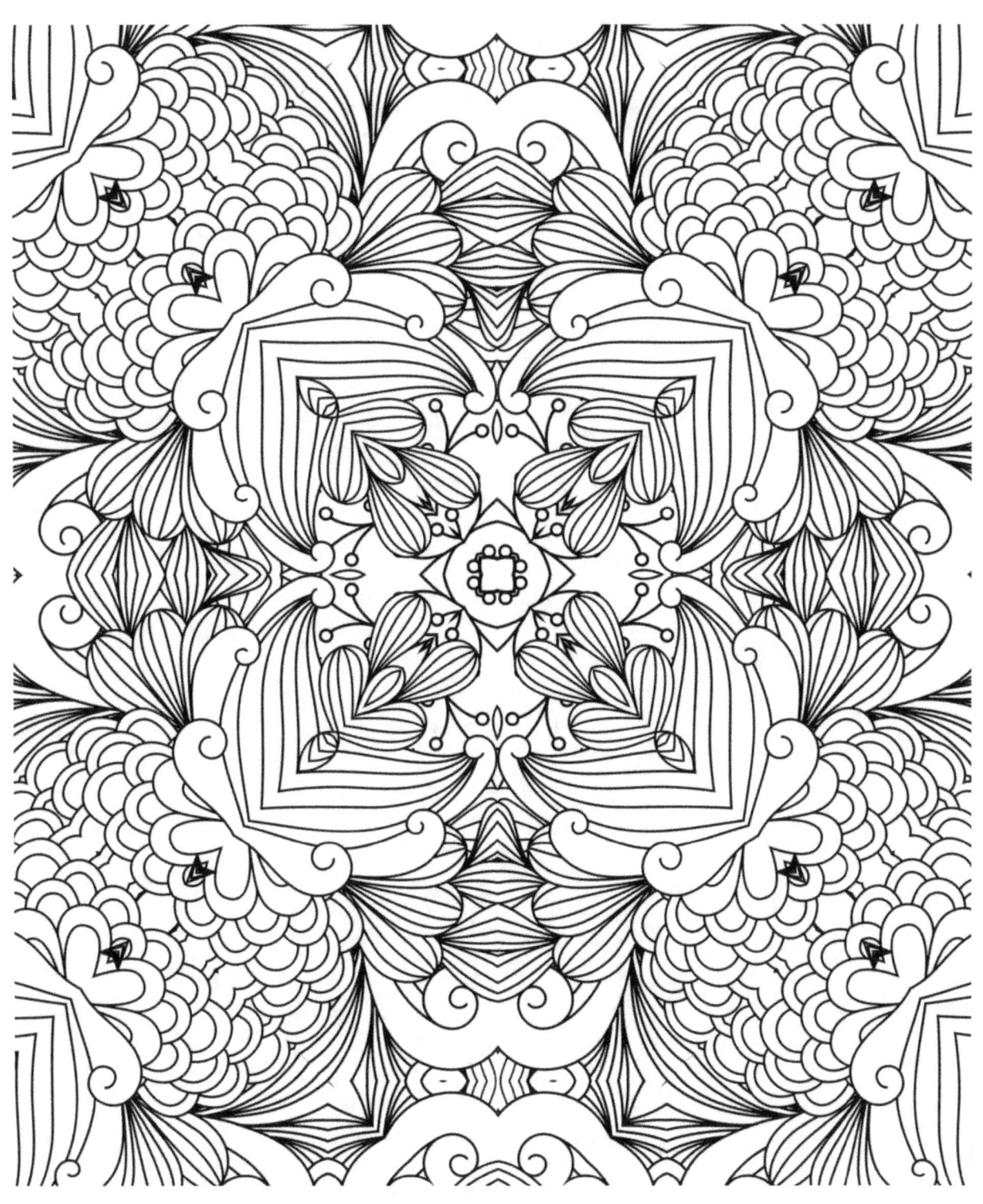

I can do all this through Him who gives me strength.

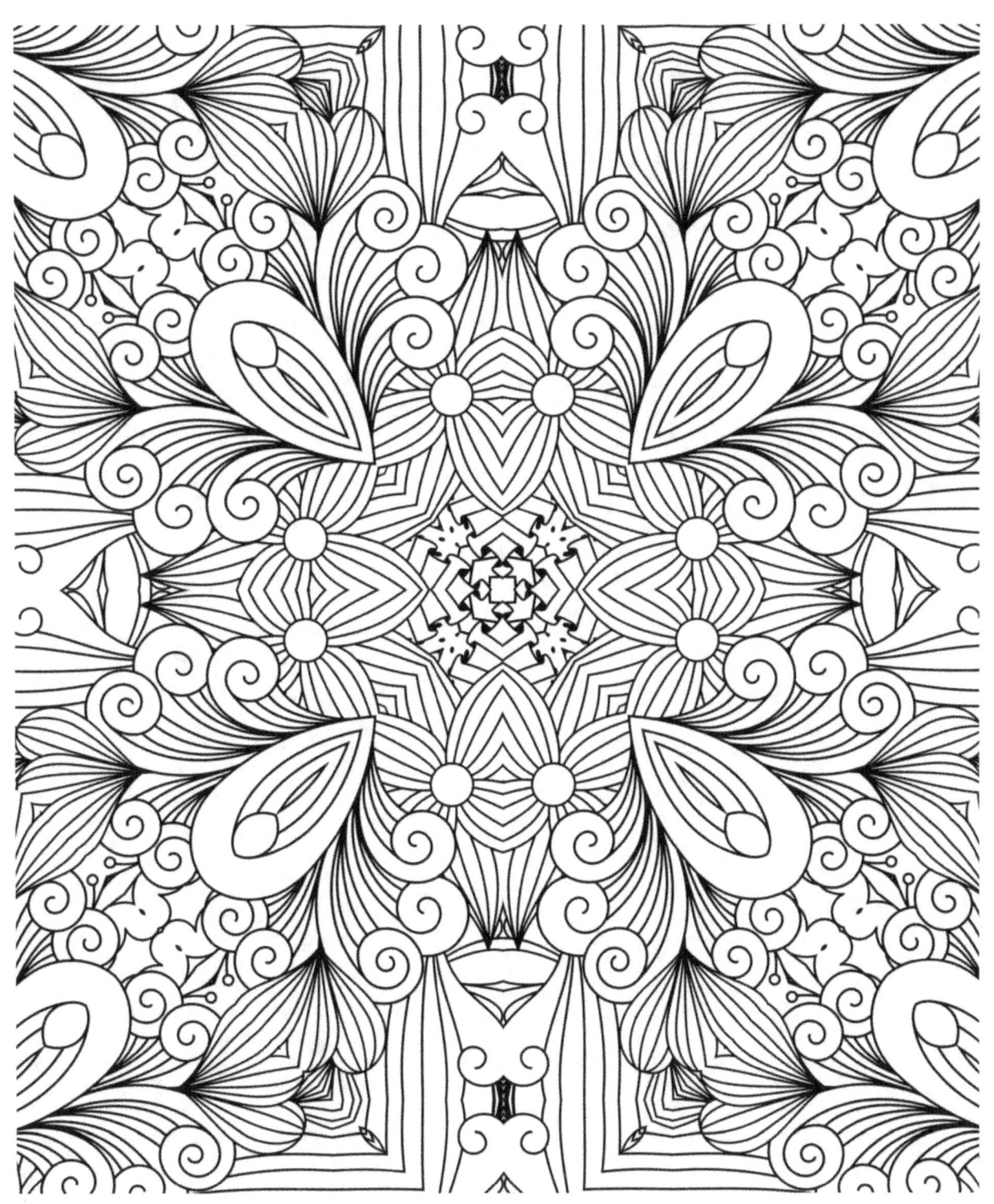

give thanks in all circumstances.

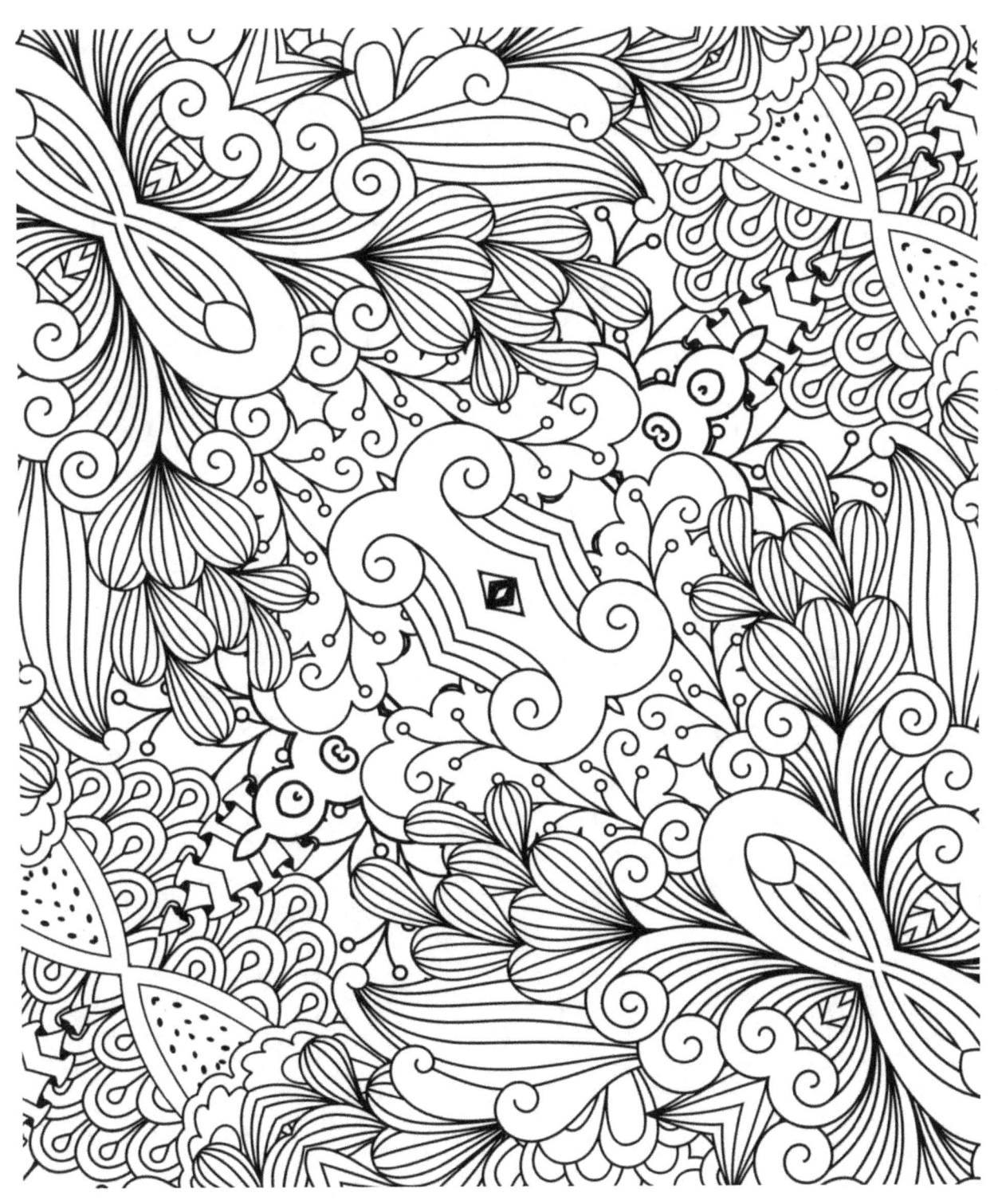

Discover beauty in everyone.

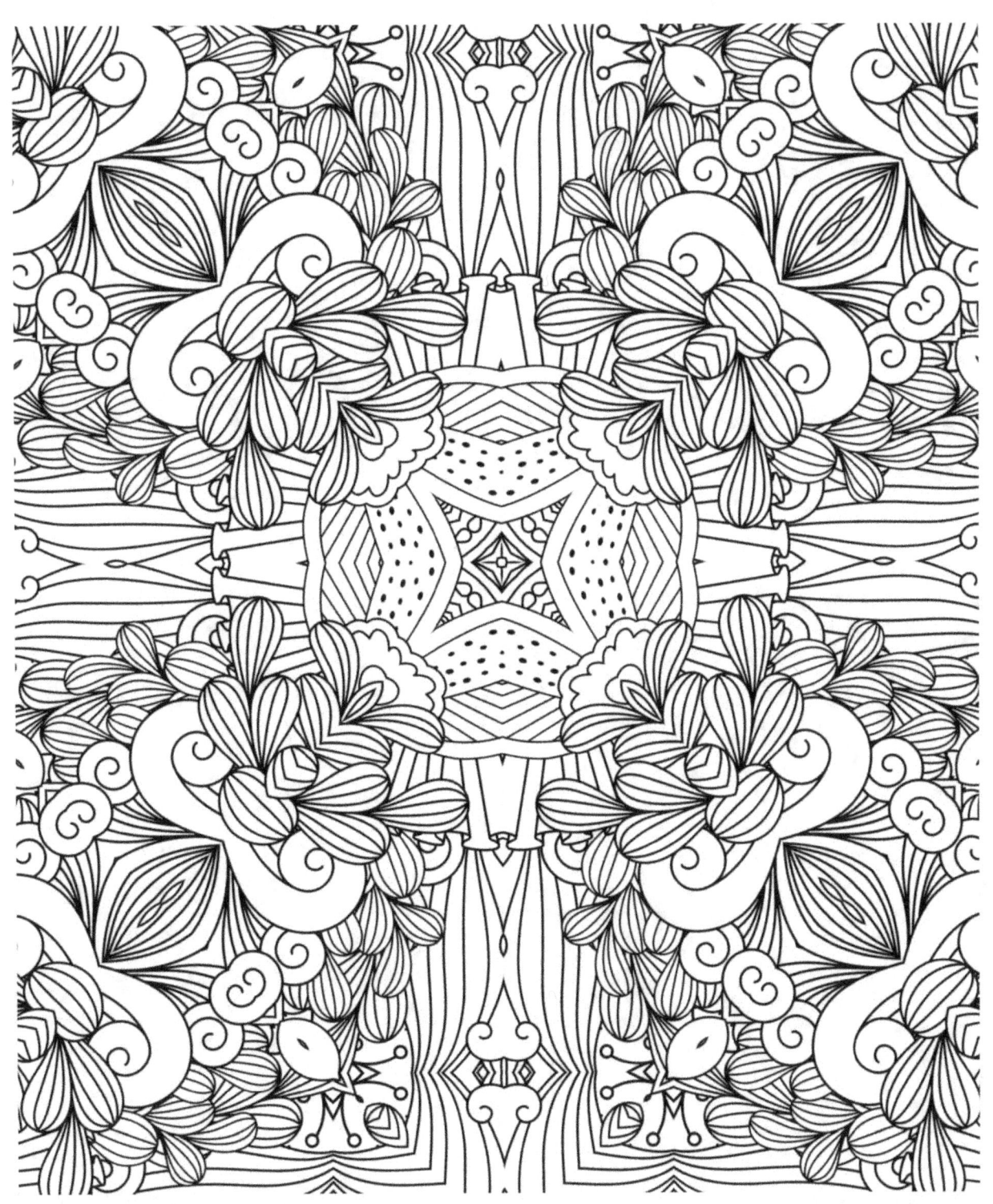

For physical training is of some value, but godliness has value for all things.

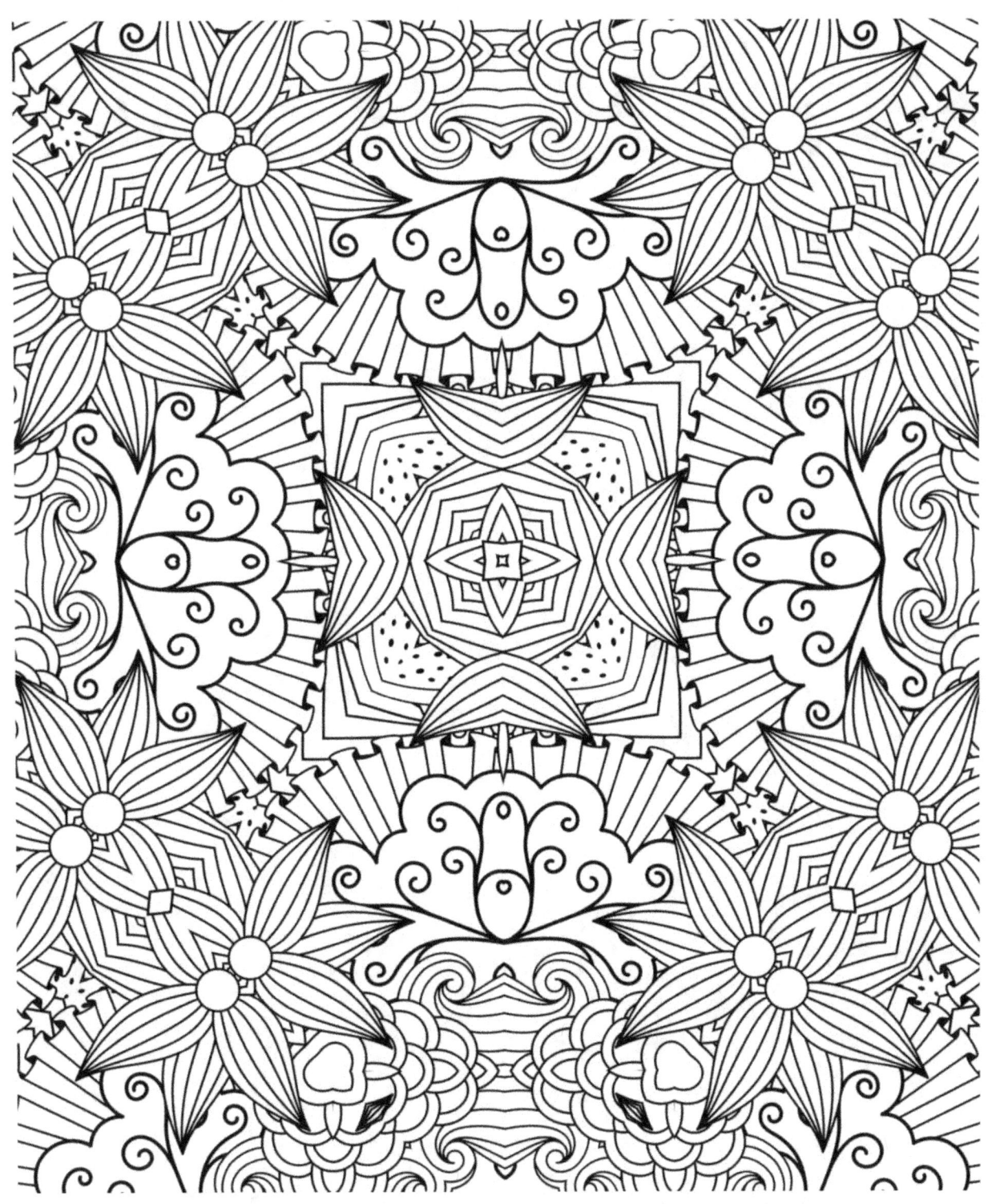

Now faith is confidence in what we hope for and assurance about what we do not see.

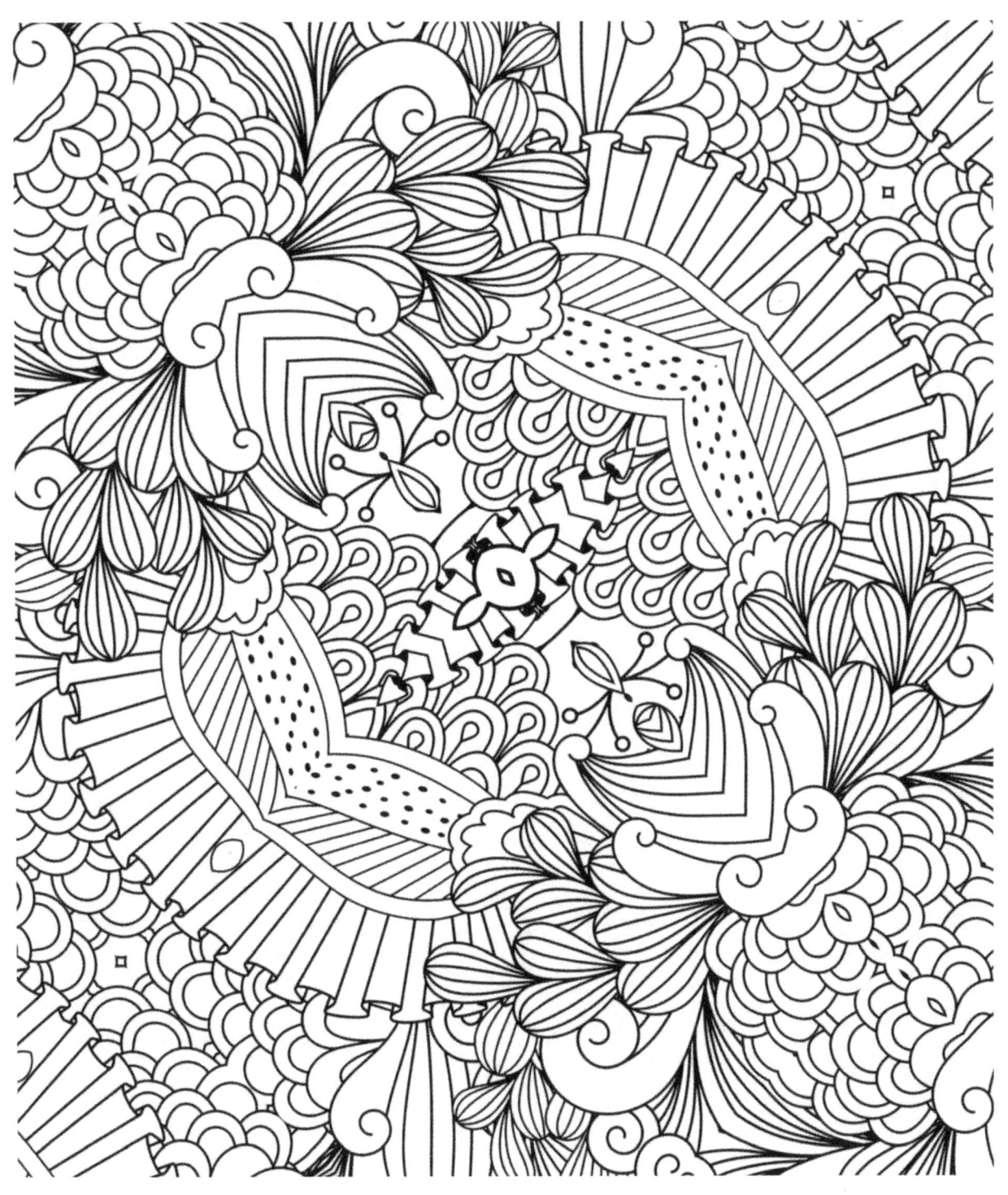

Come to me, all you who are weary and burdened, and I will give you rest.

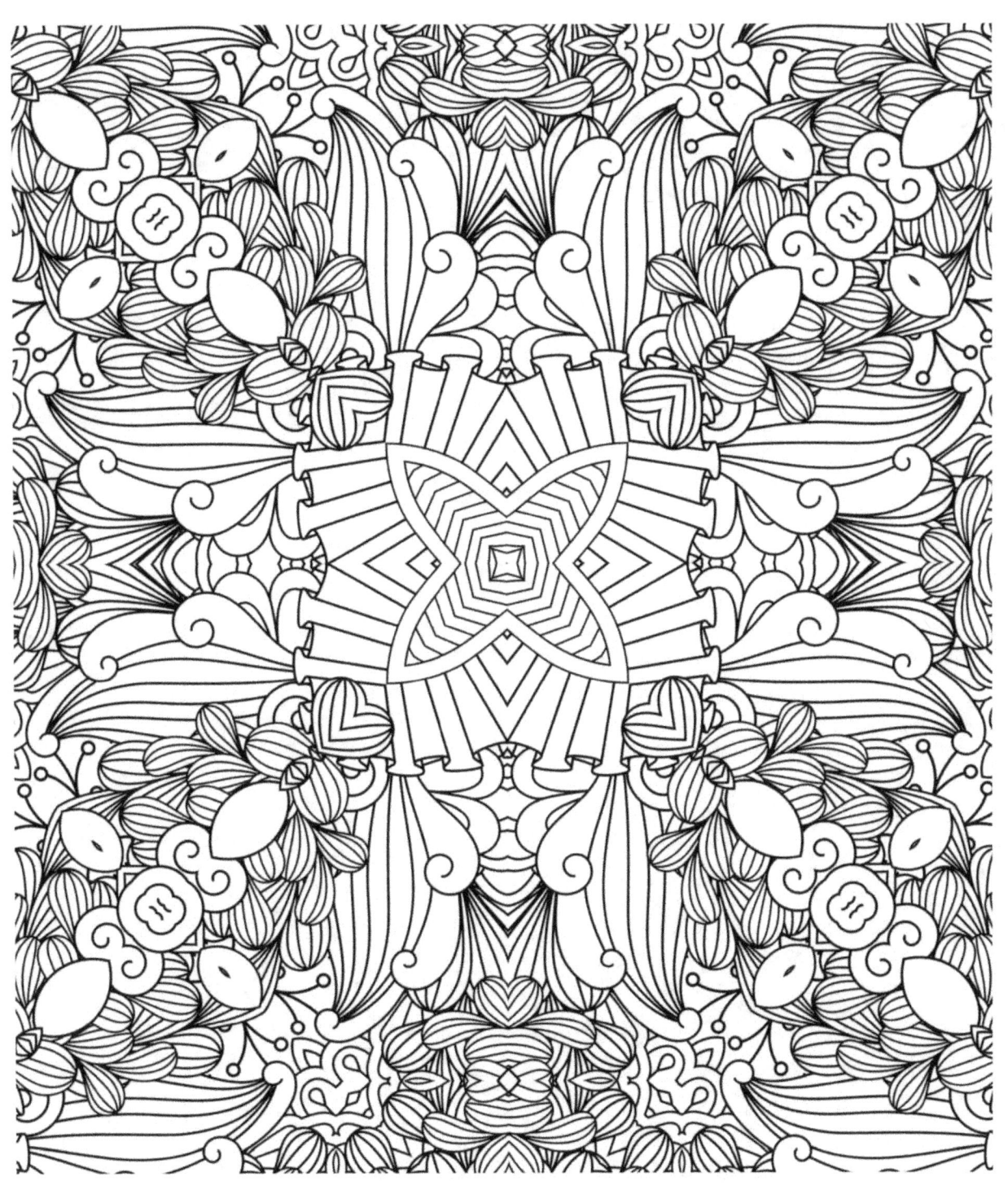

Arise, shine, for your light has come, and the glory of the Lord rises upon you.

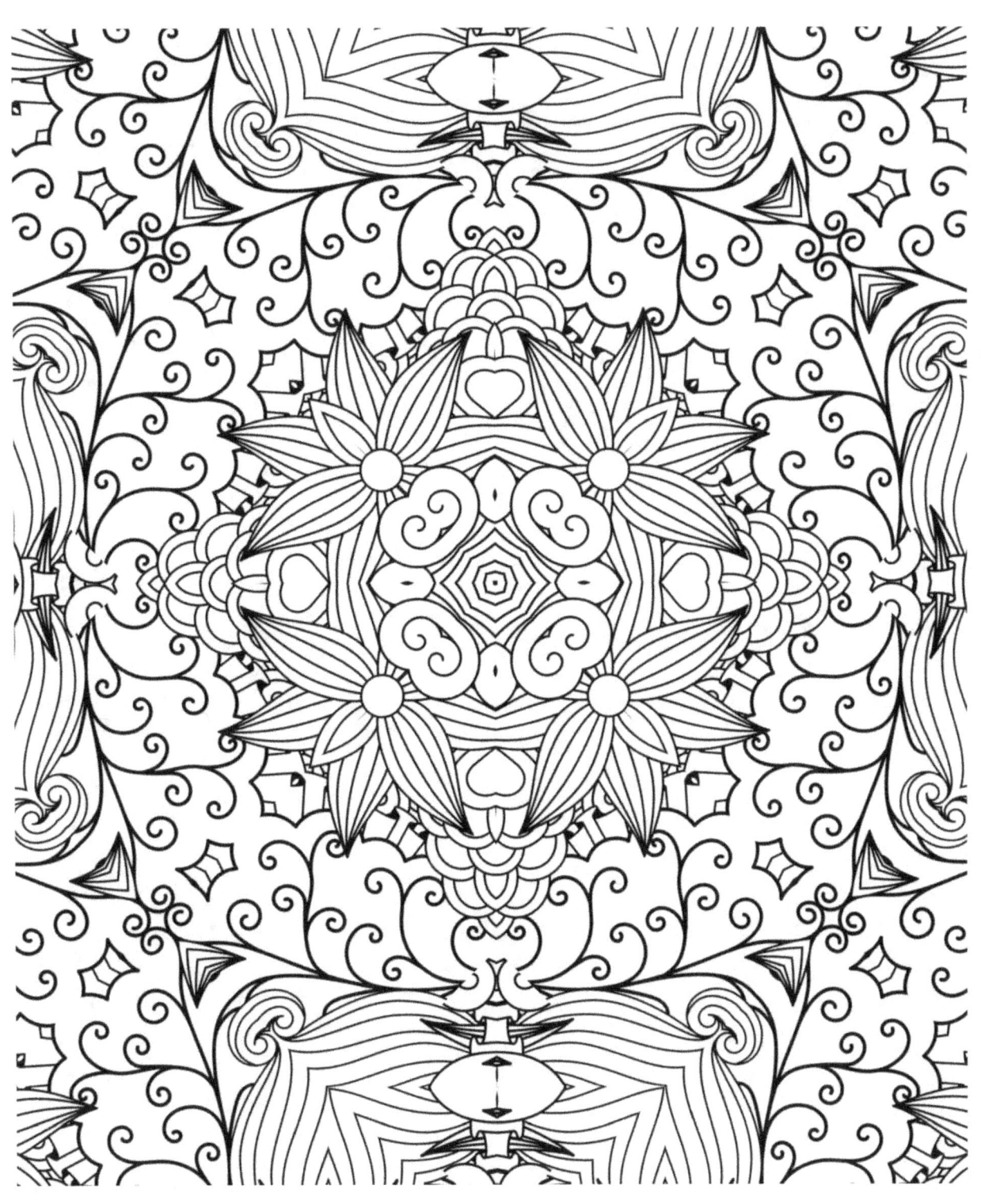

He has made everything beautiful in its time.

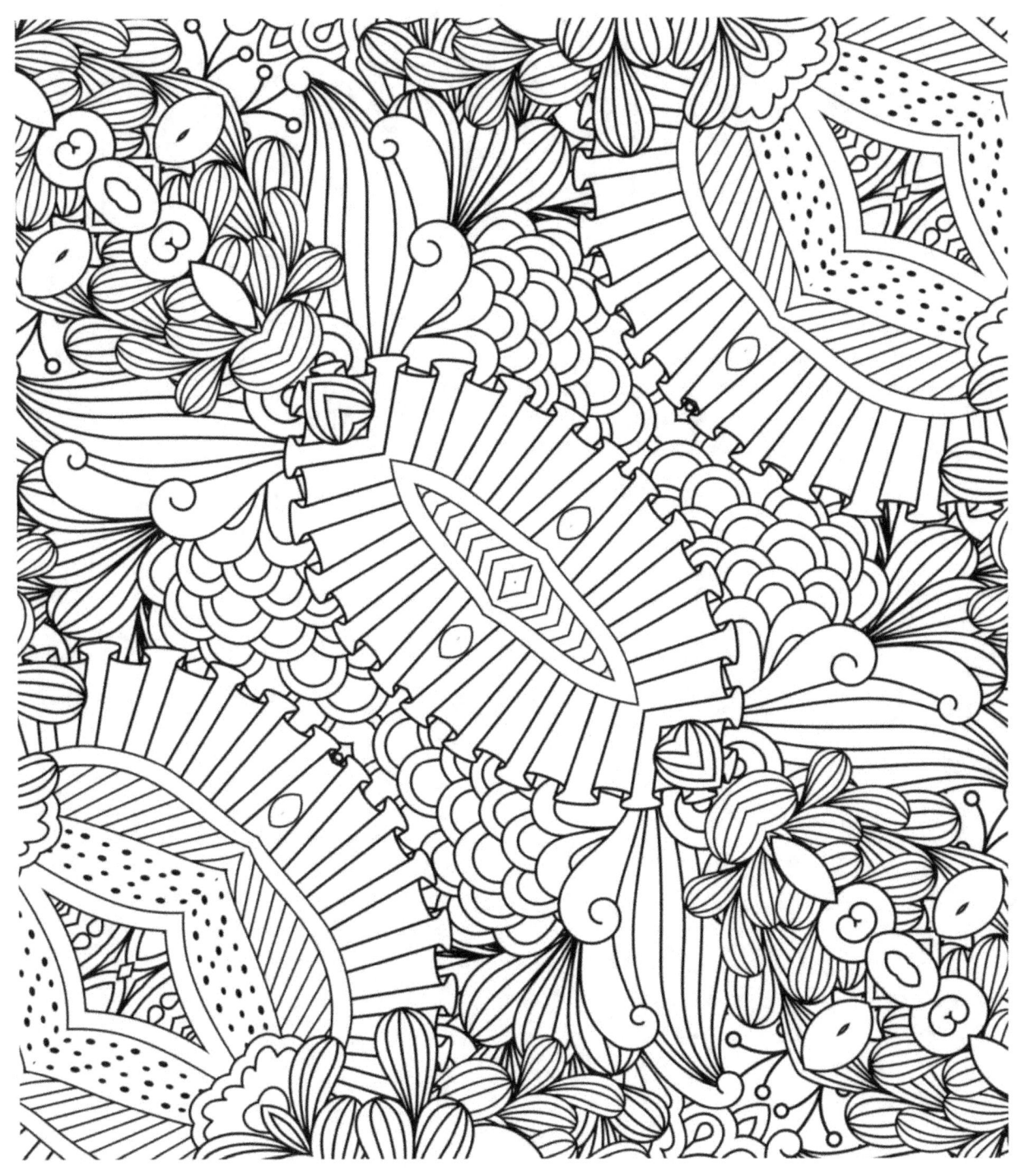

The grass withers and the flowers fall, but the word of our God endures forever.

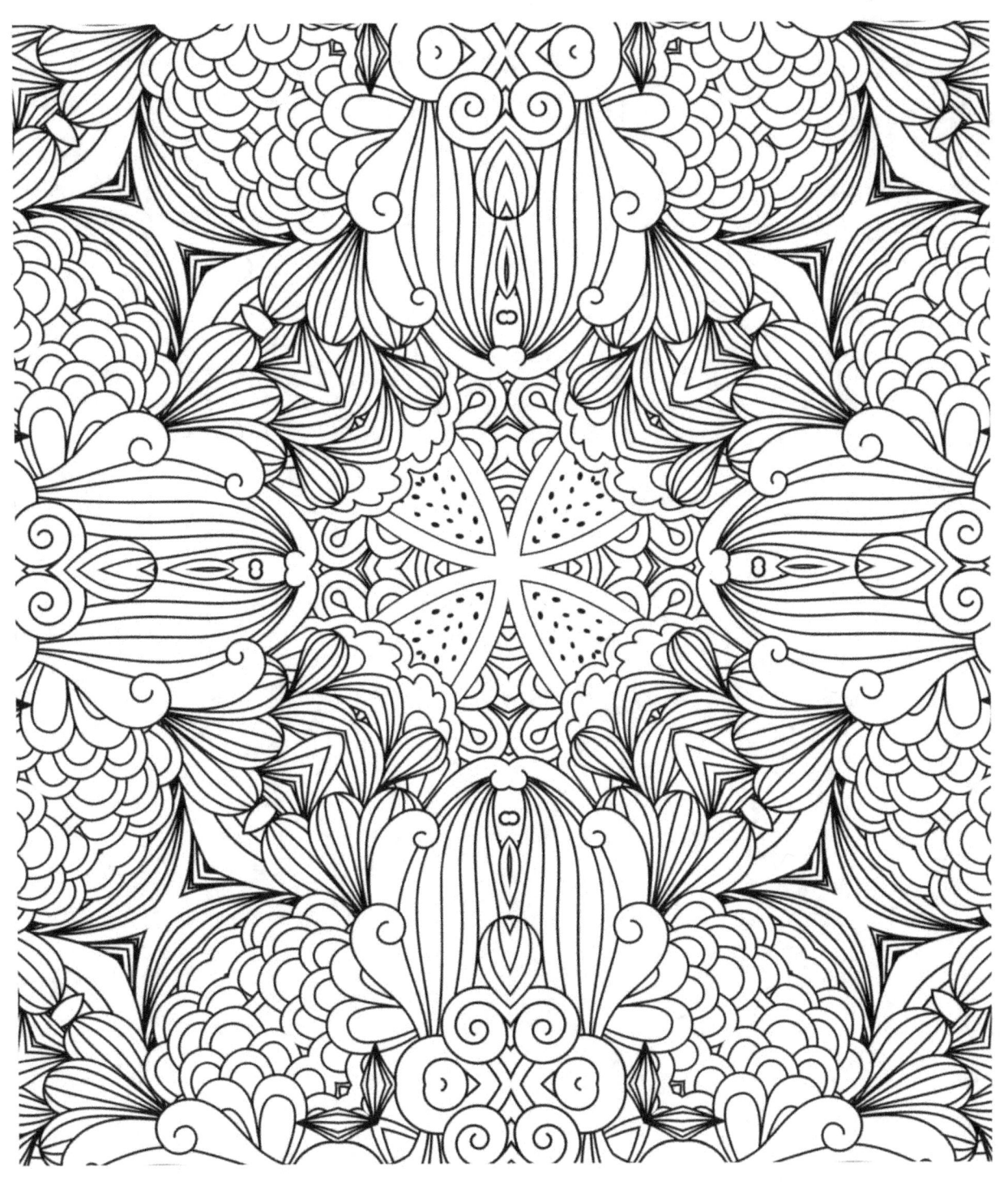

For we are God's handiwork, created in Christ Jesus to do good works.

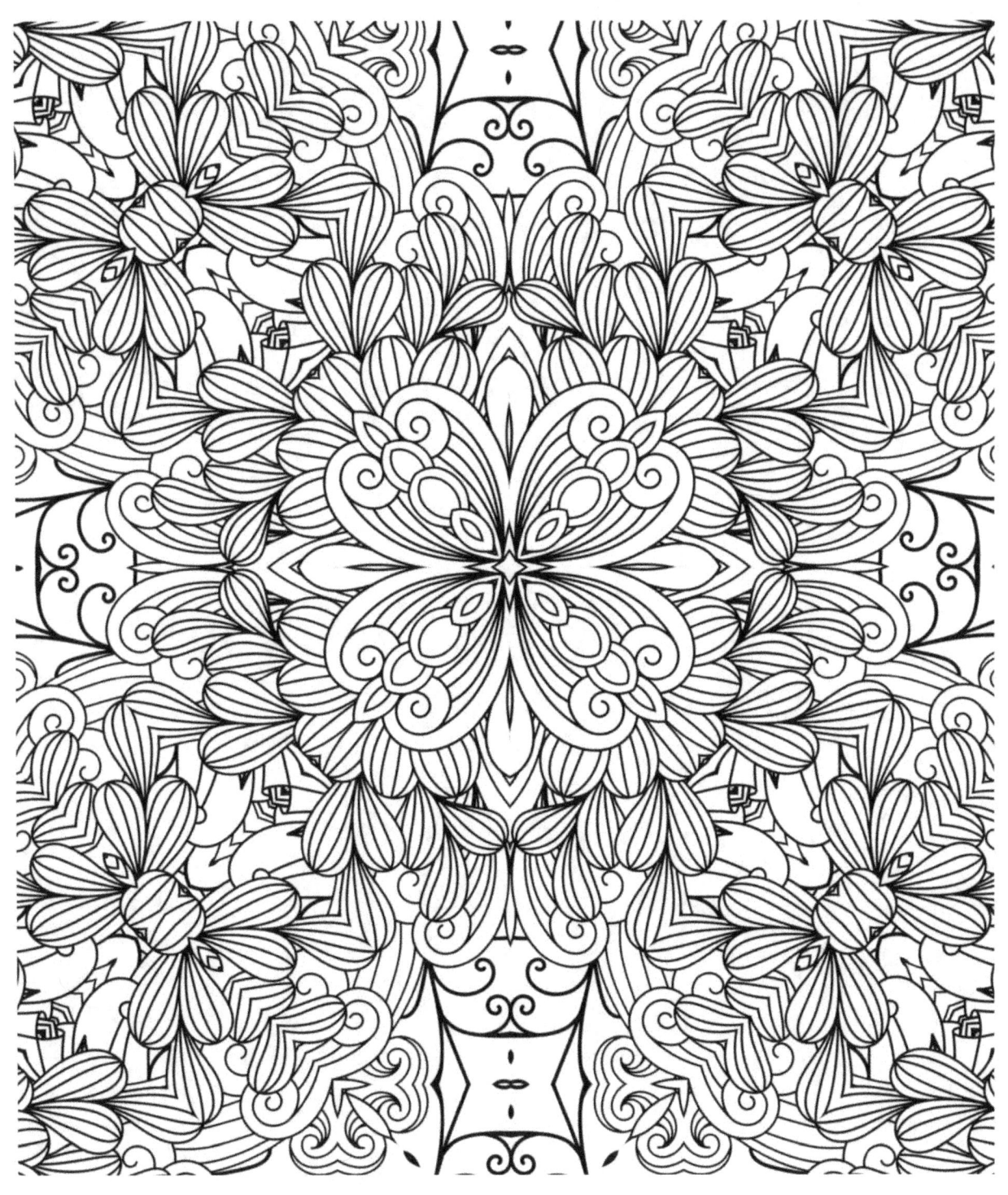

For every house is built by someone, but God is the builder of everything.

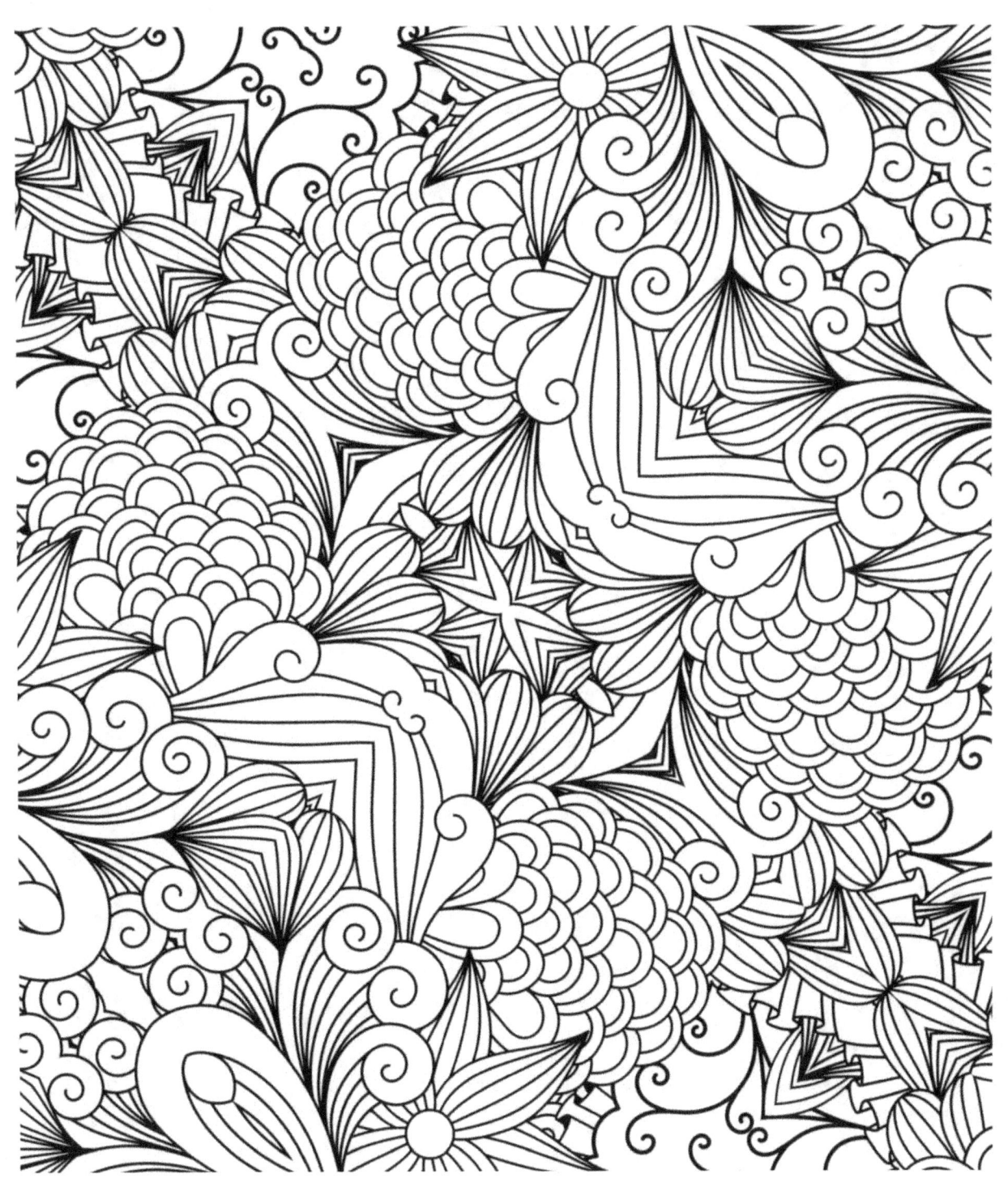

For the creation waits in eager expectation for the children of God to be revealed.

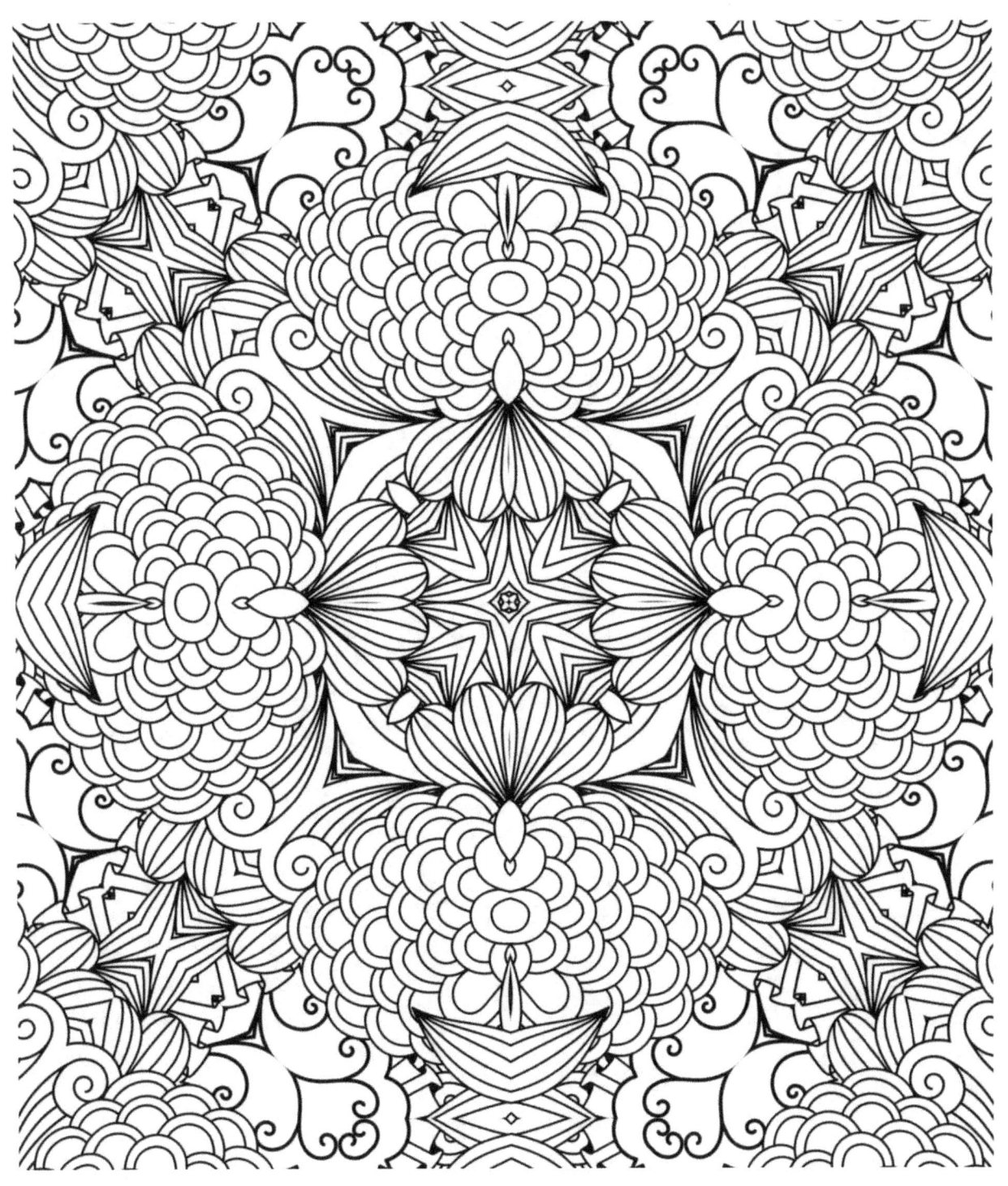

The Lord has done it this very day; let us rejoice today and be glad.

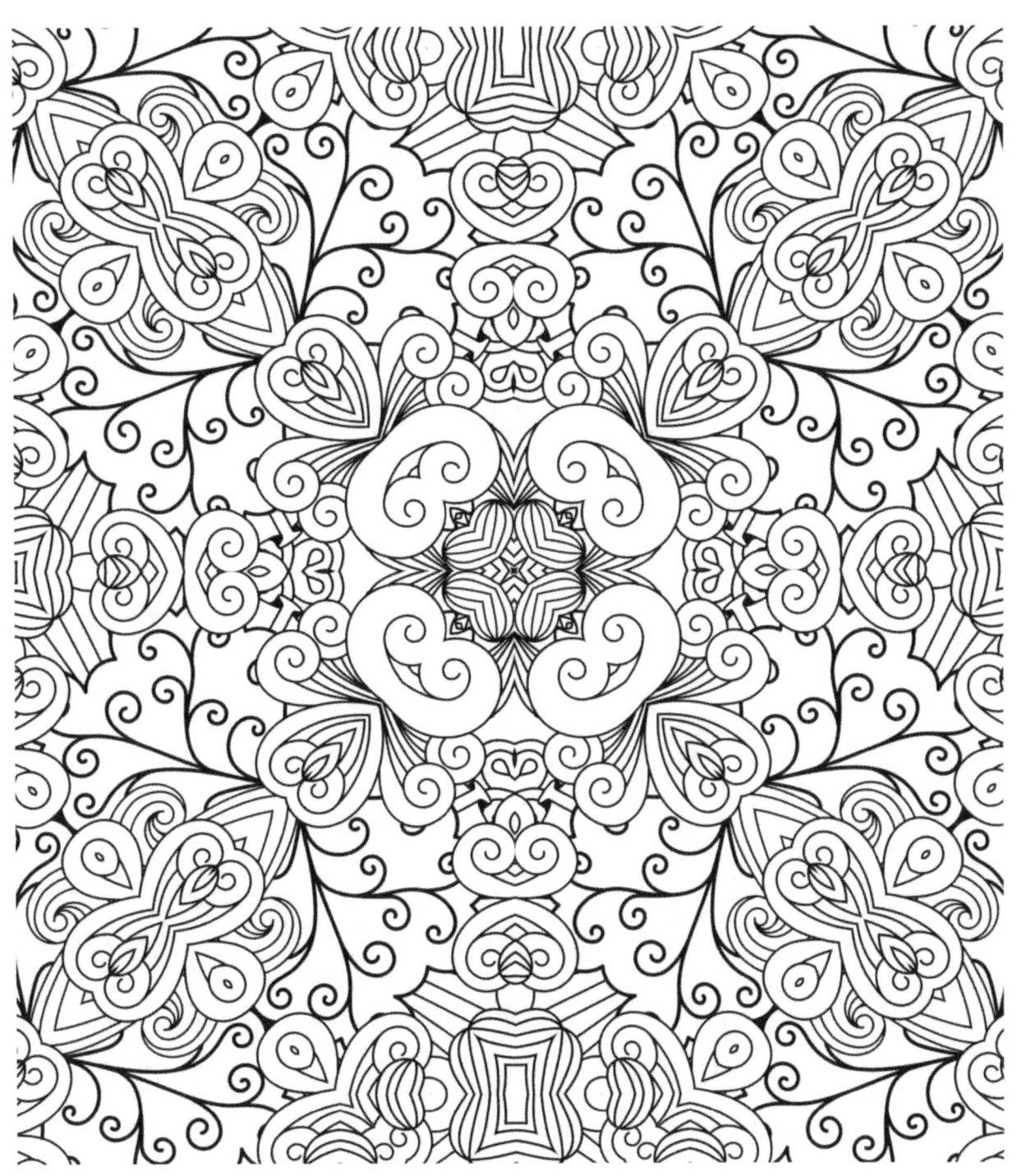

Therefore, if anyone is in Christ, the new creation has come: The old has gone, the new is here!

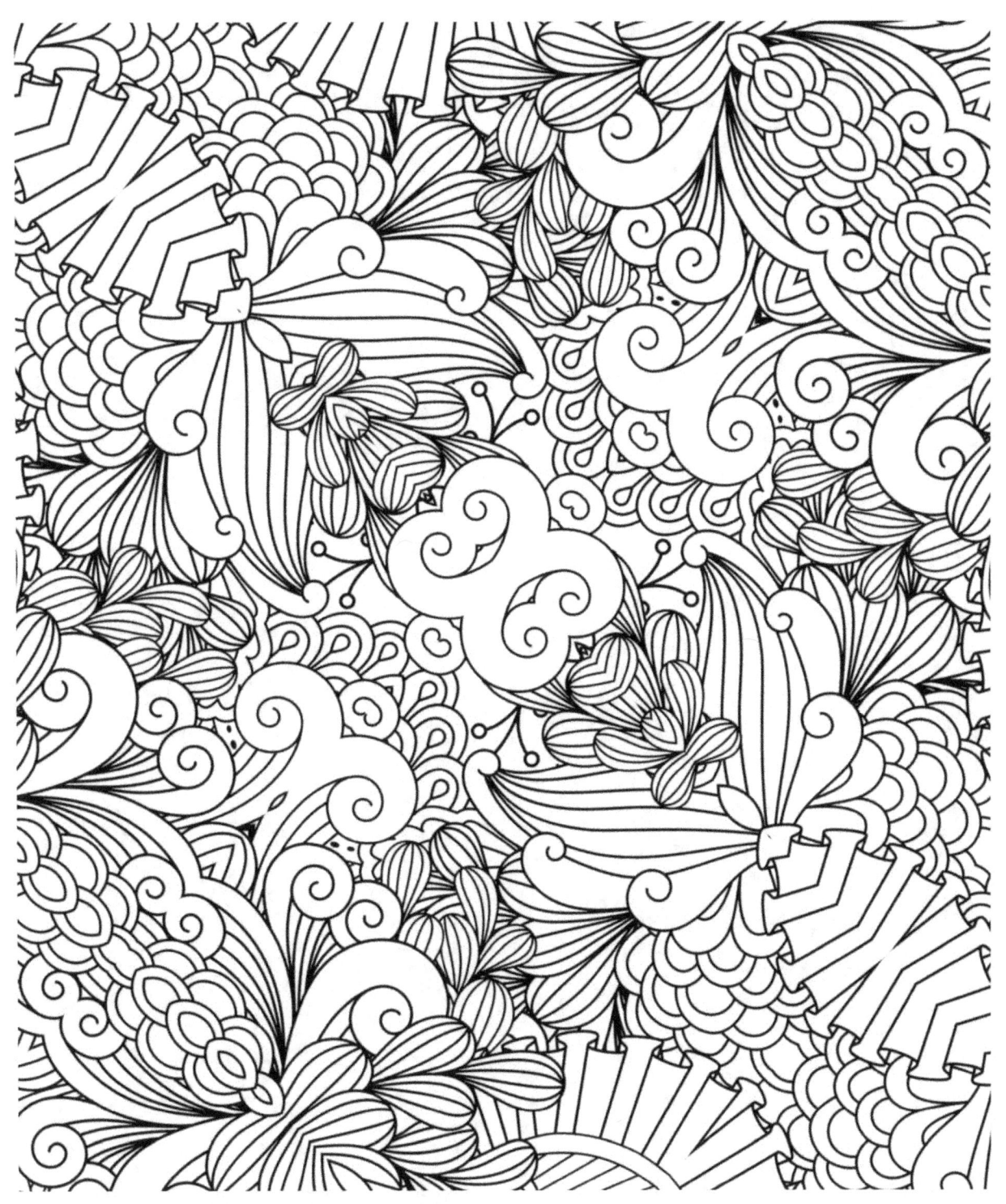

Our help is in the name of the Lord, the Maker of heaven and earth.

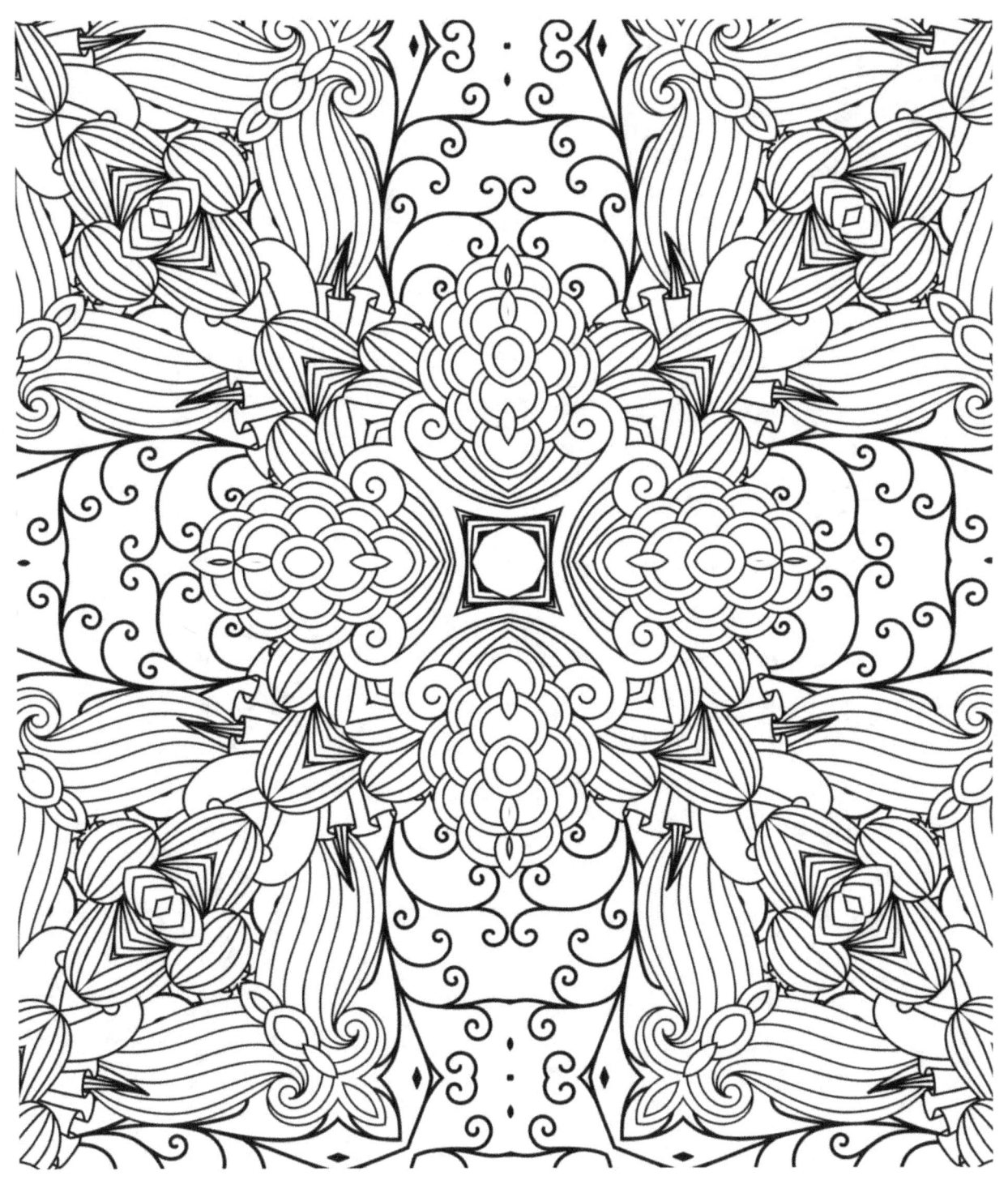

Come, let us bow down in worship, let us kneel before the Lord our Maker.

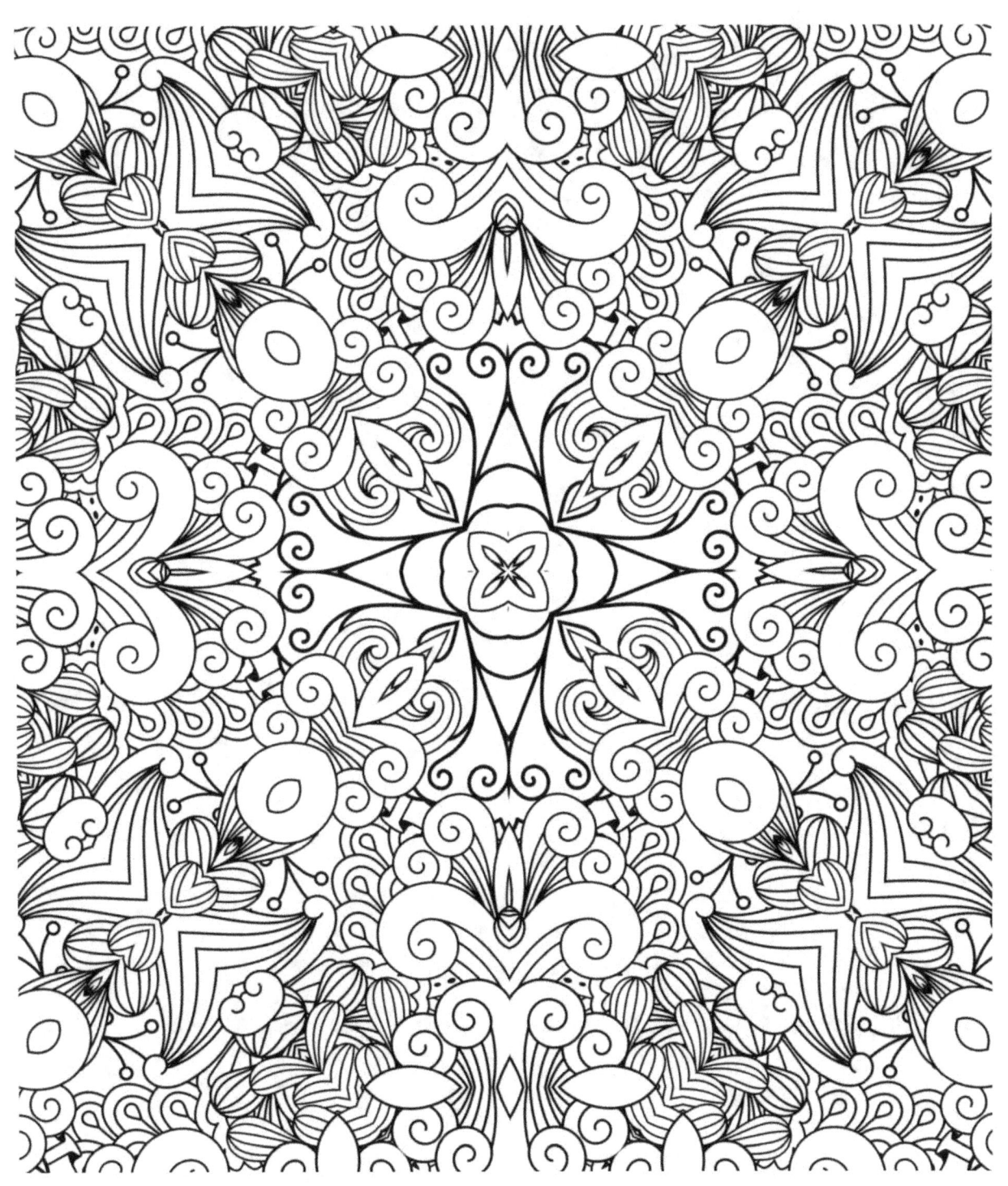

He has made everything beautiful in its time. He has also set eternity in the human heart.

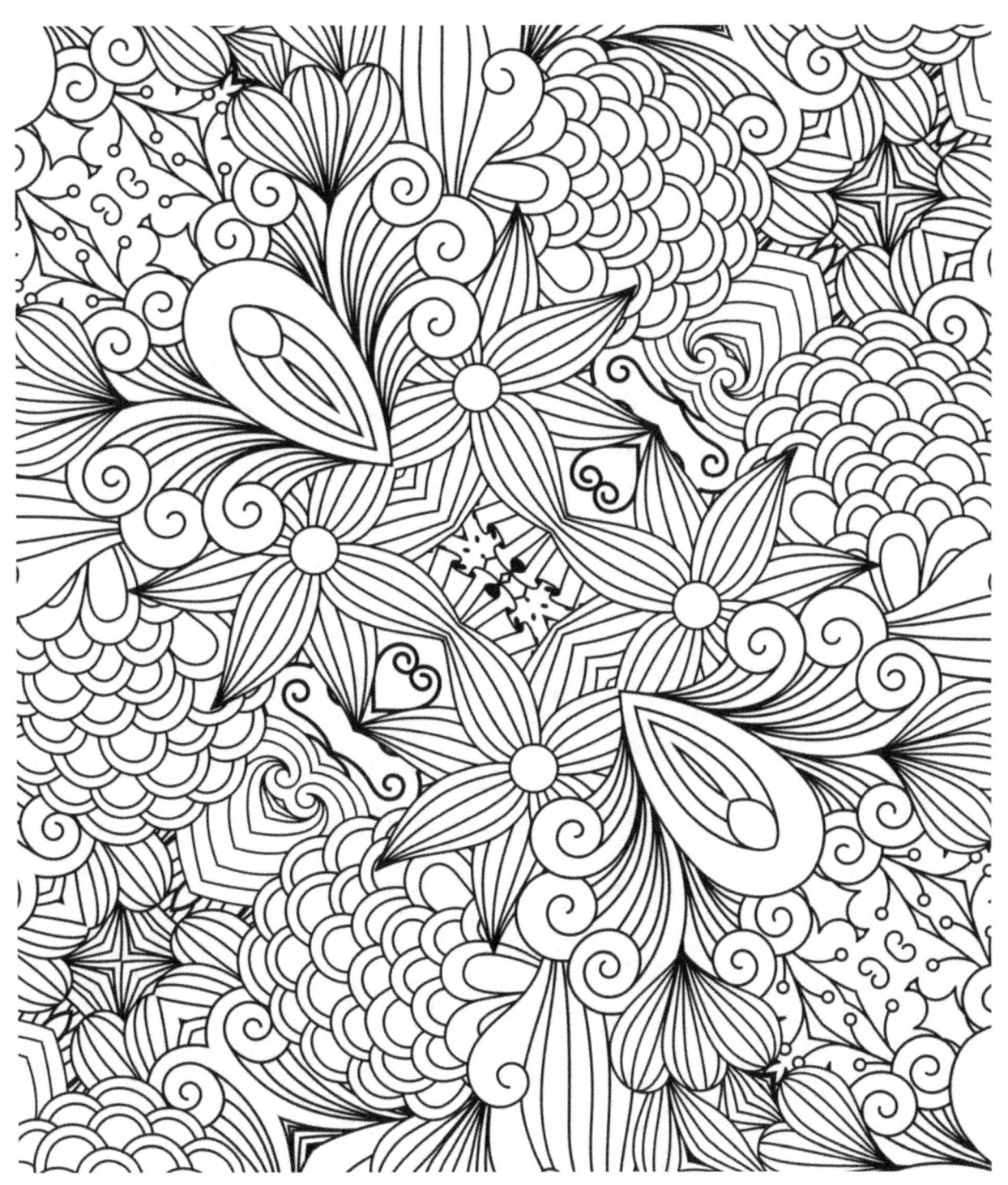

Through him all things were made; without him nothing was made that has been made.

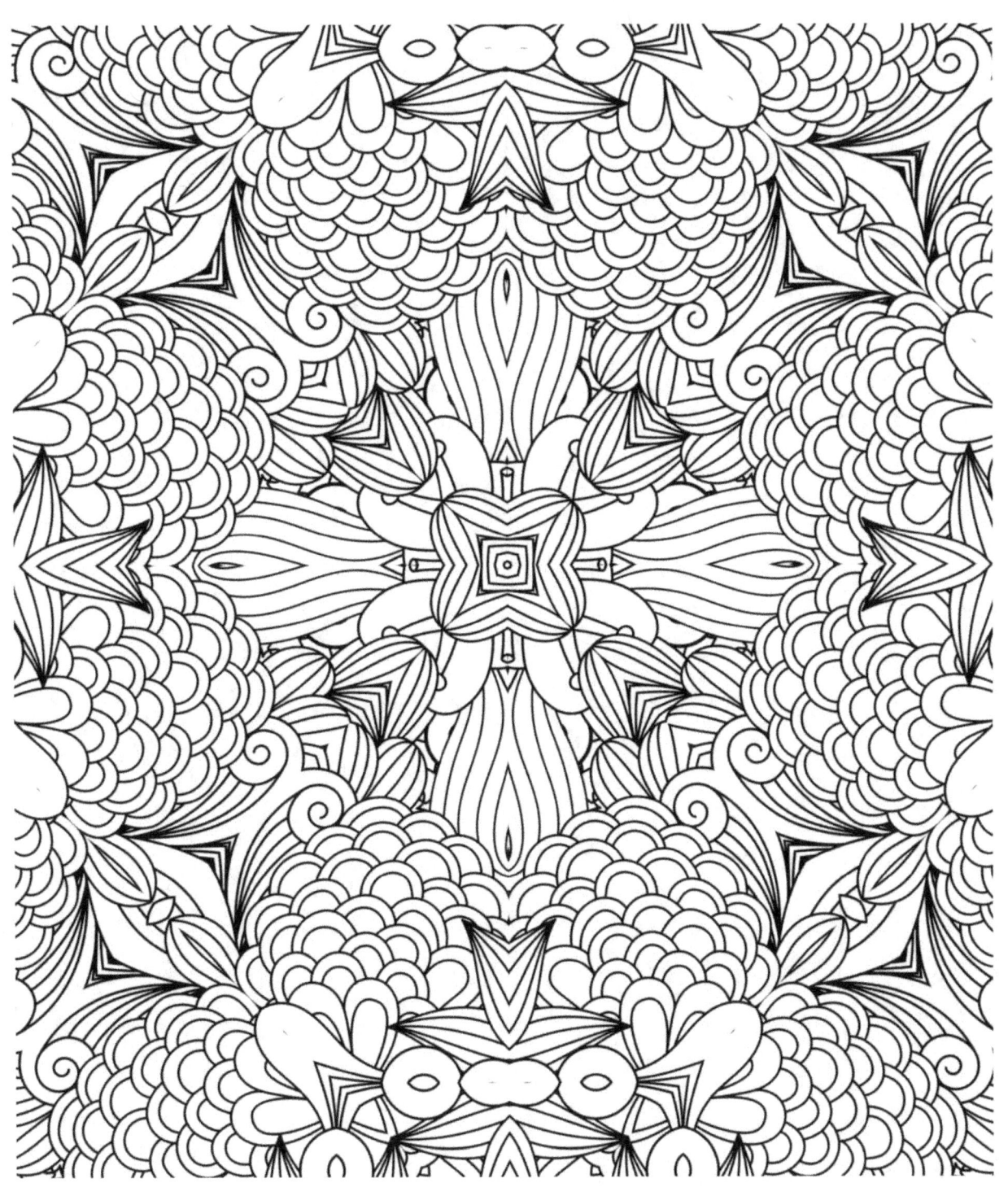

And God said, "Let there be light." and there was light.

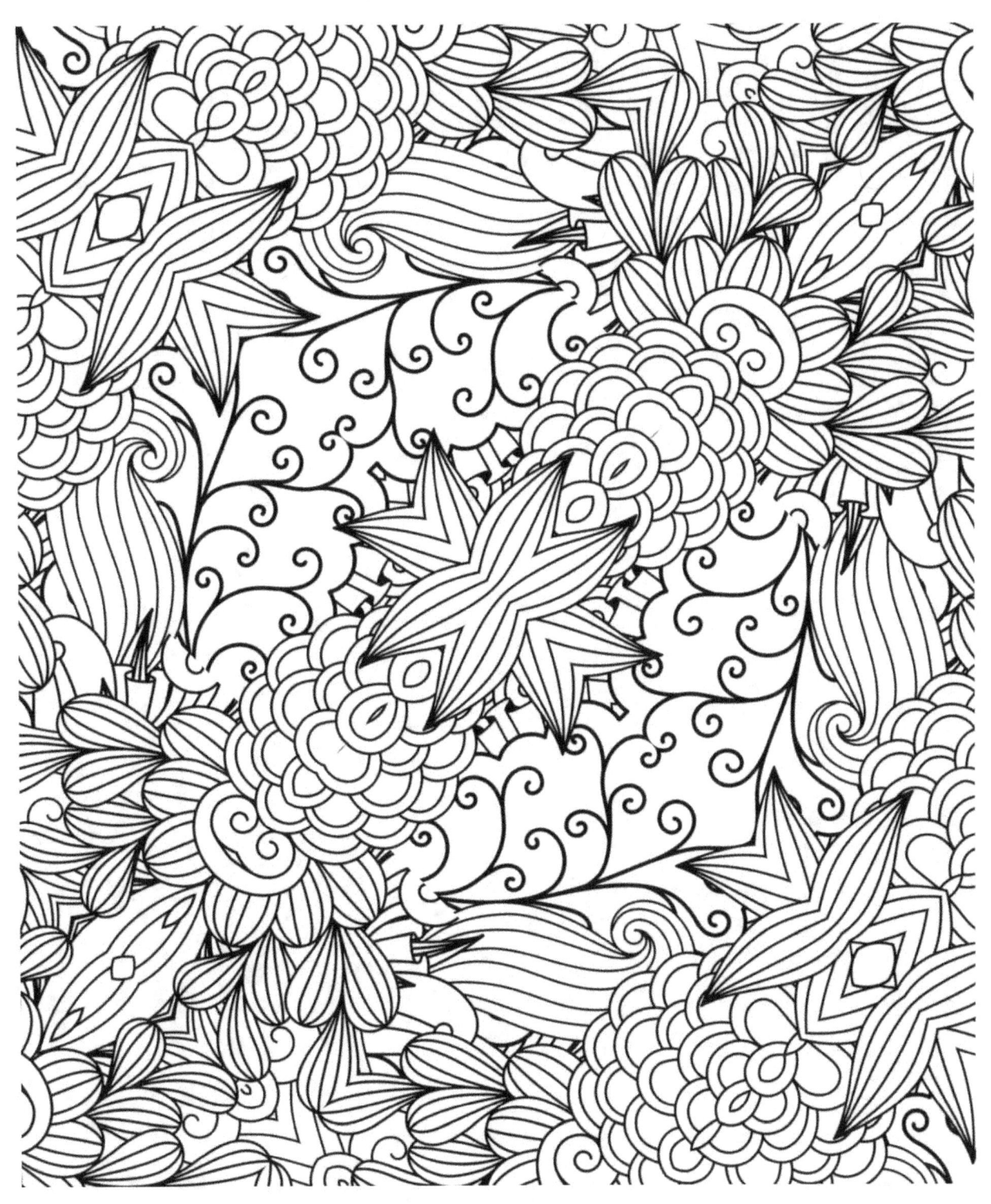

For we live by faith, not by sight.

My flesh and my heart may fail, but God is the strength of my heart.

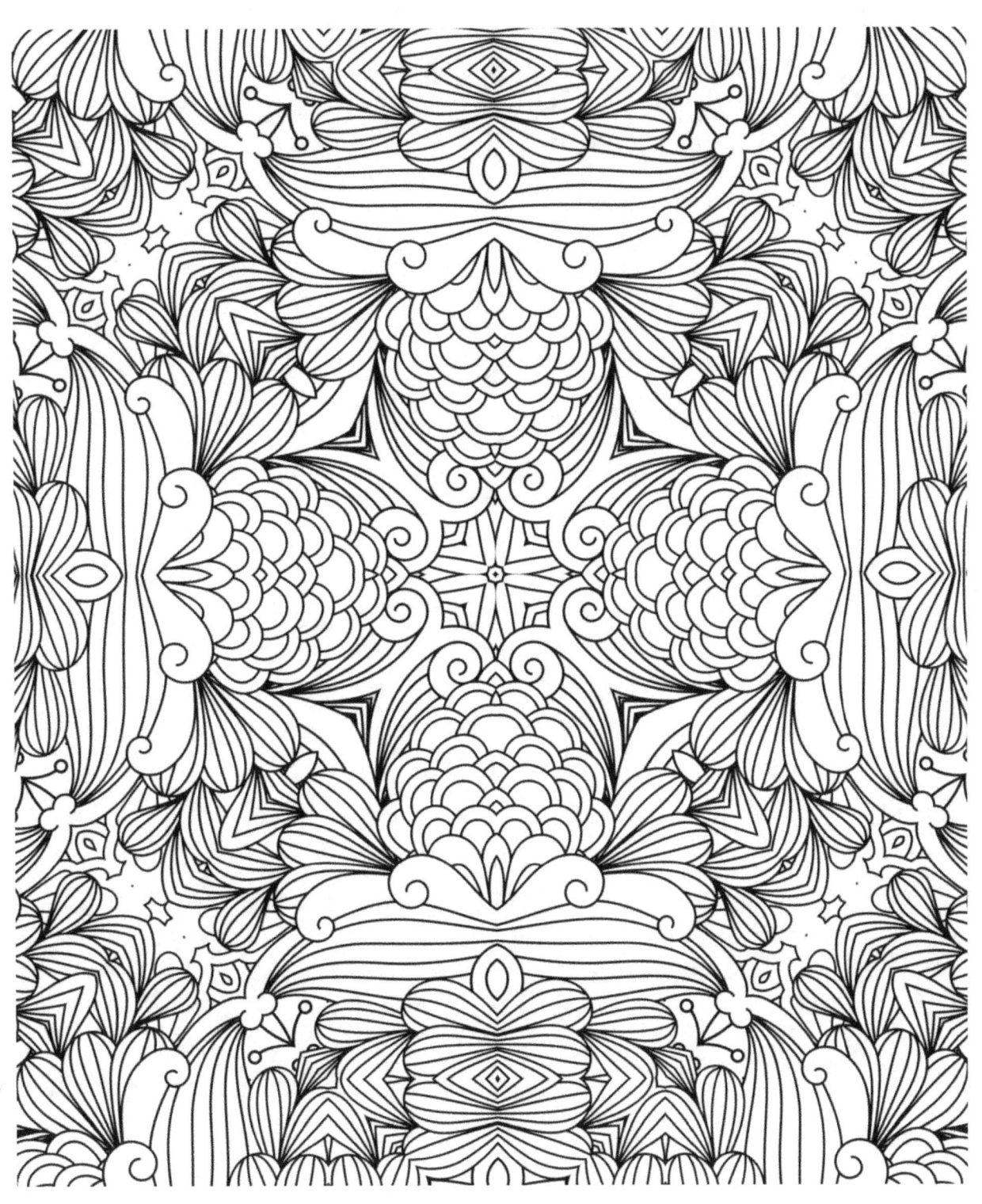

Above all else, guard your heart.

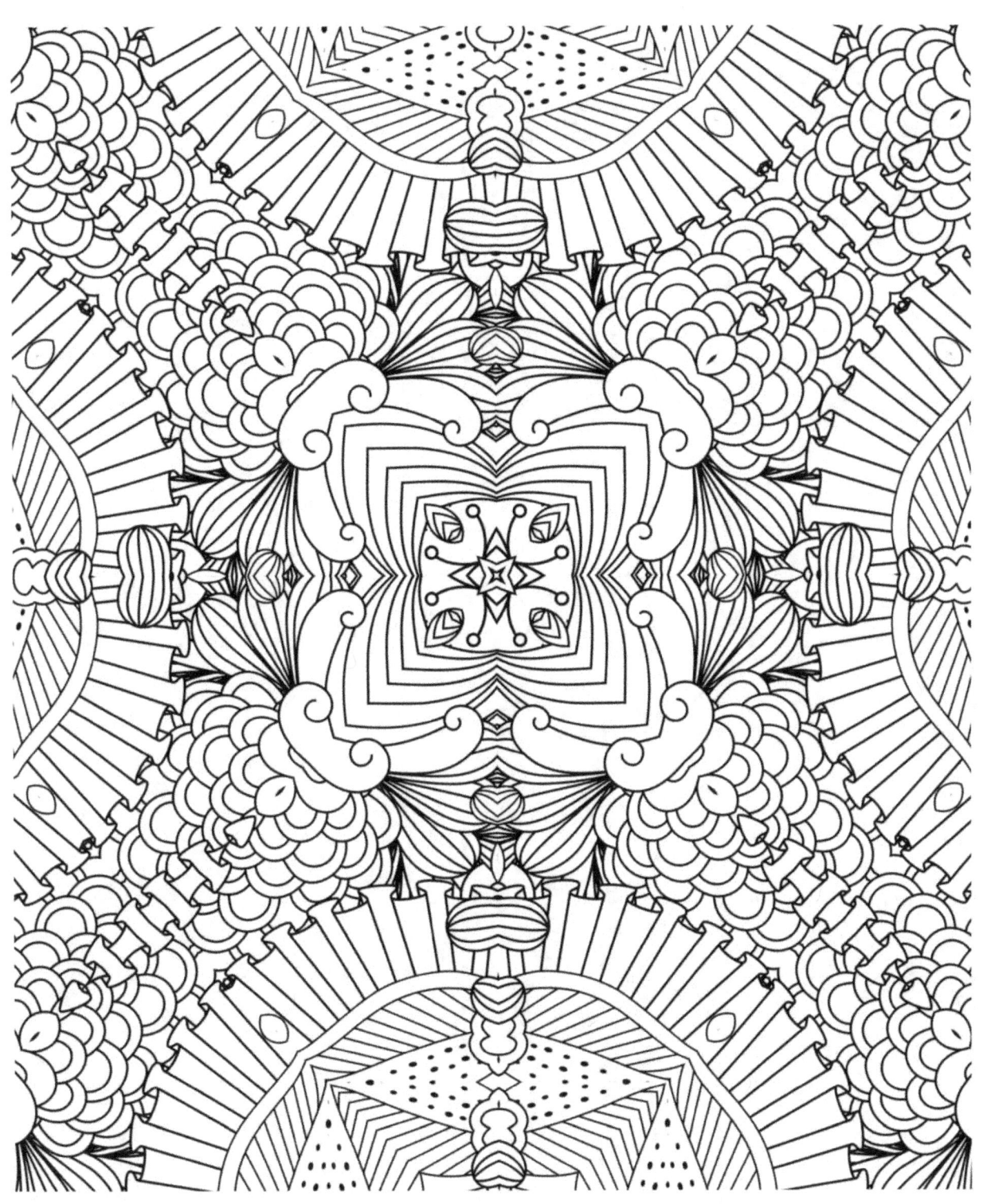

Be still before the Lord and wait patiently for him.

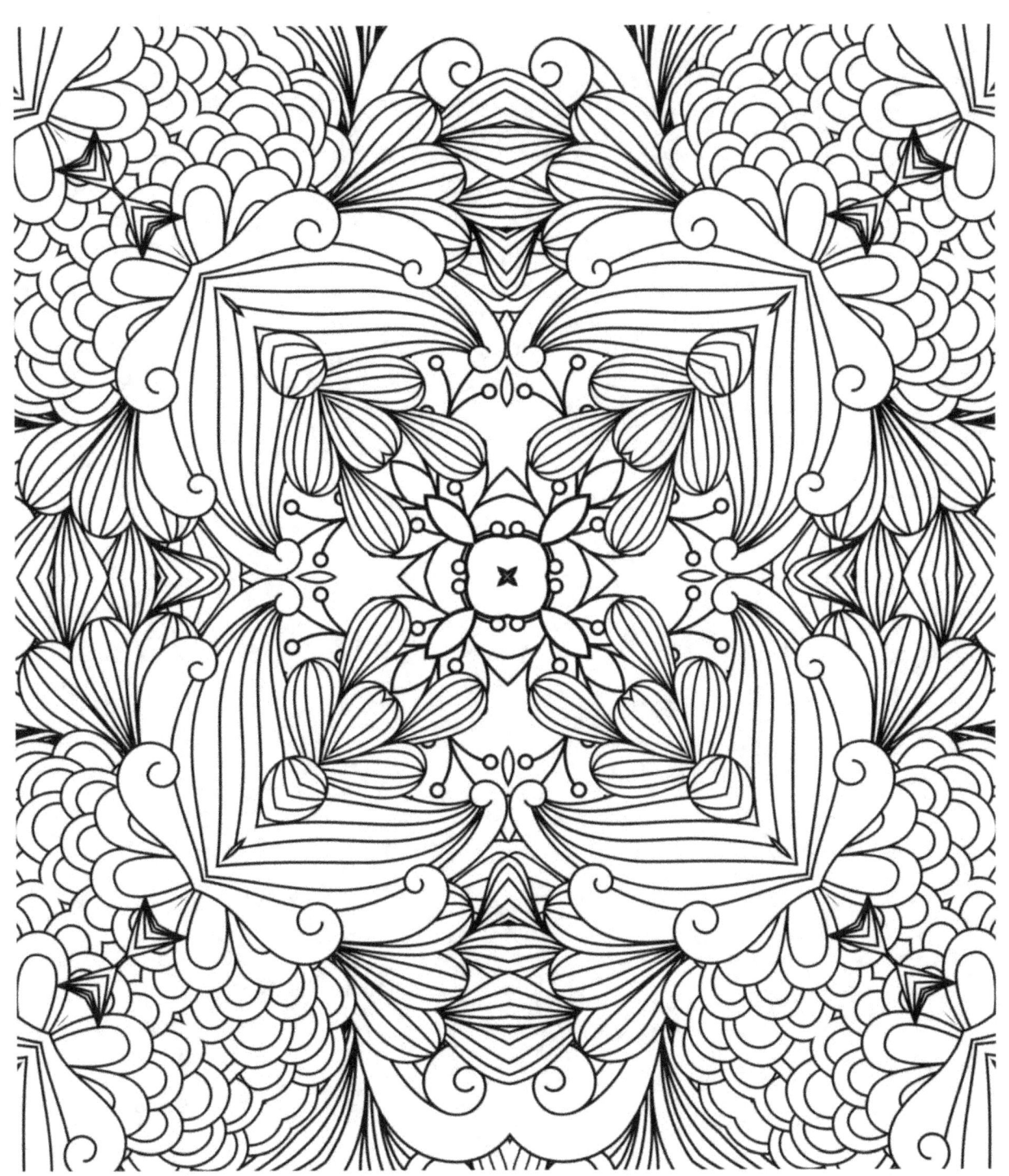

Whoever believes in me, as Scripture has said, rivers of living water will flow from within them.

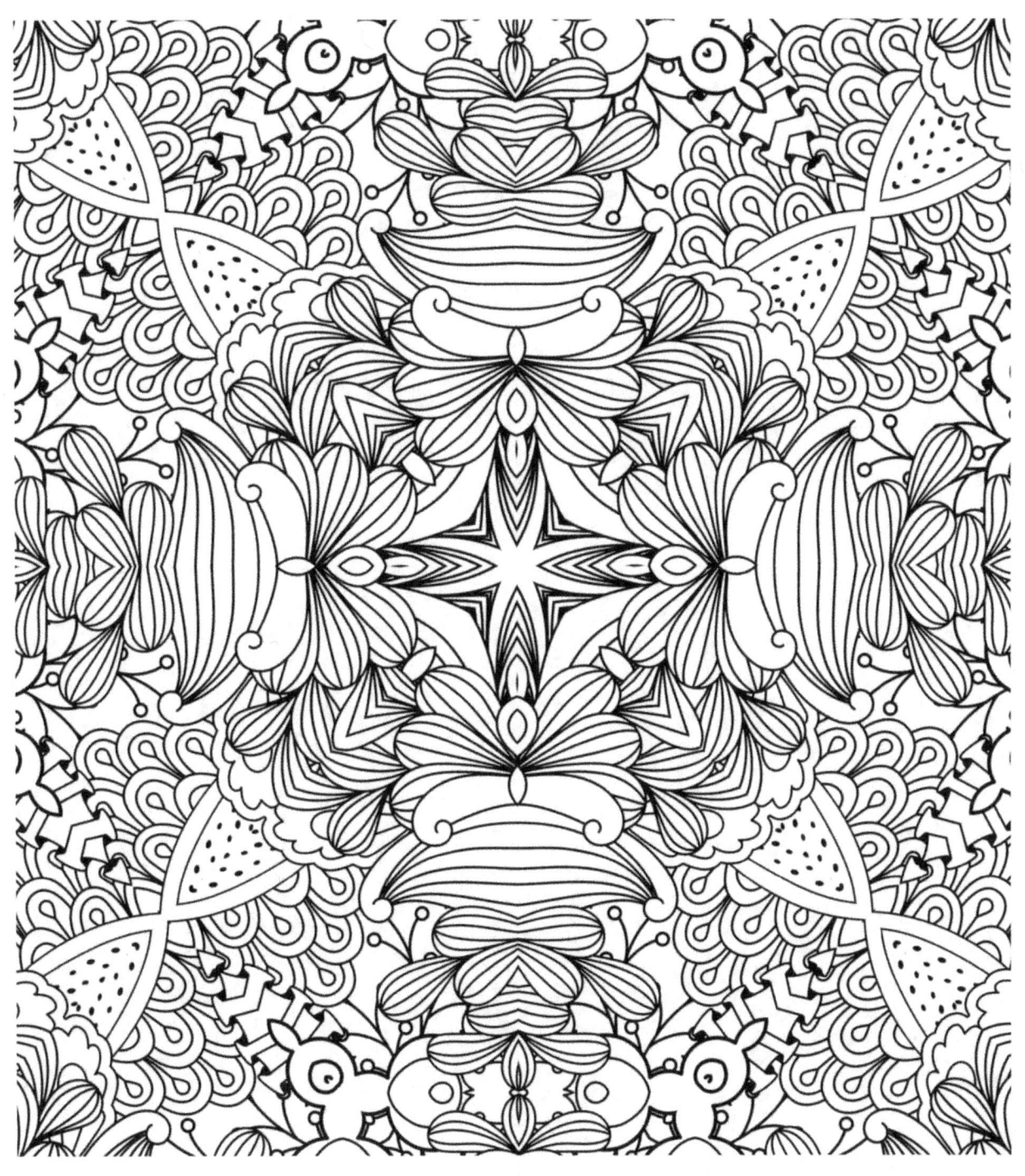

Since we live by the Spirit, let us keep in step with the Spirit.

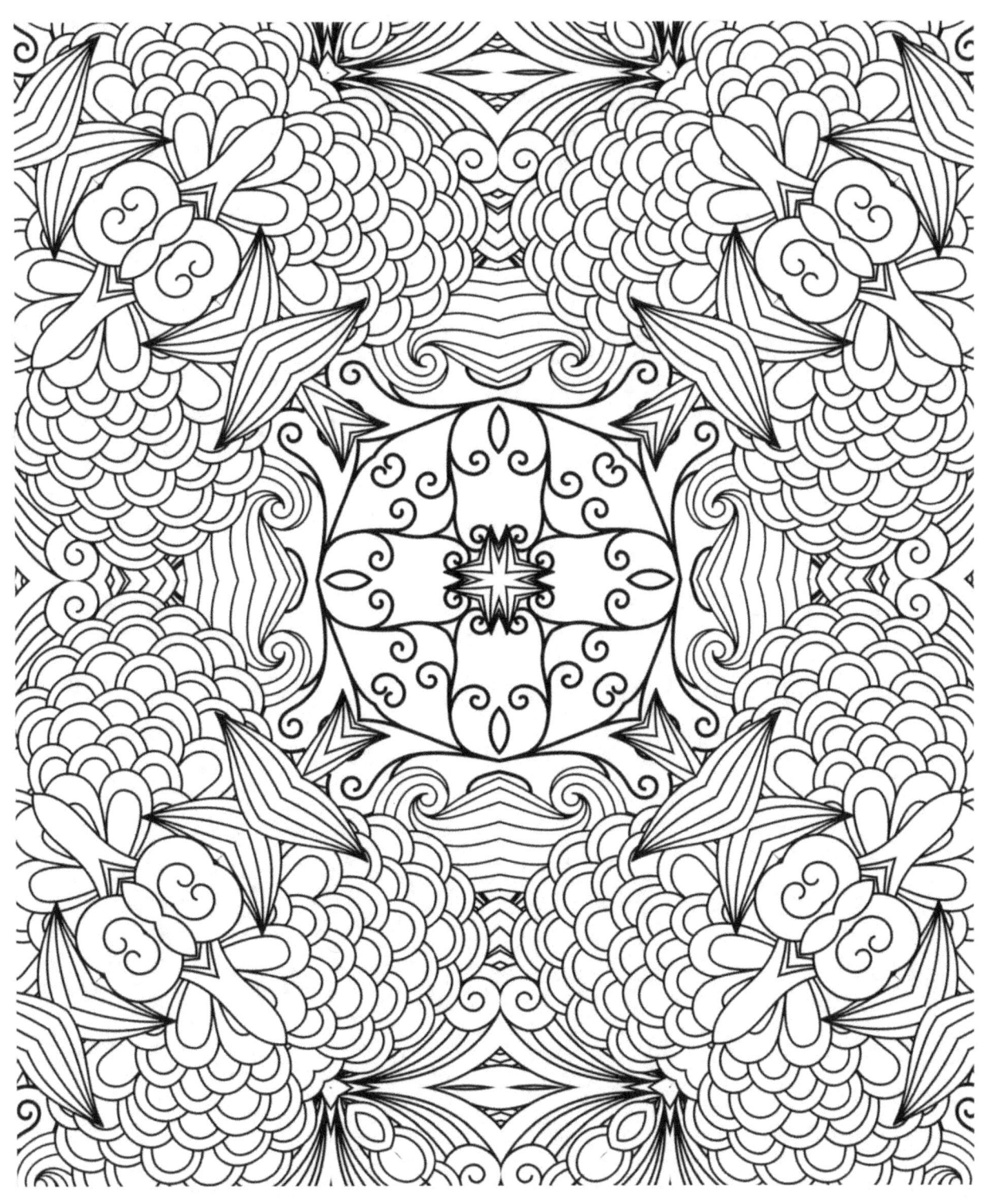

The earth is the Lord's, and everything in it.

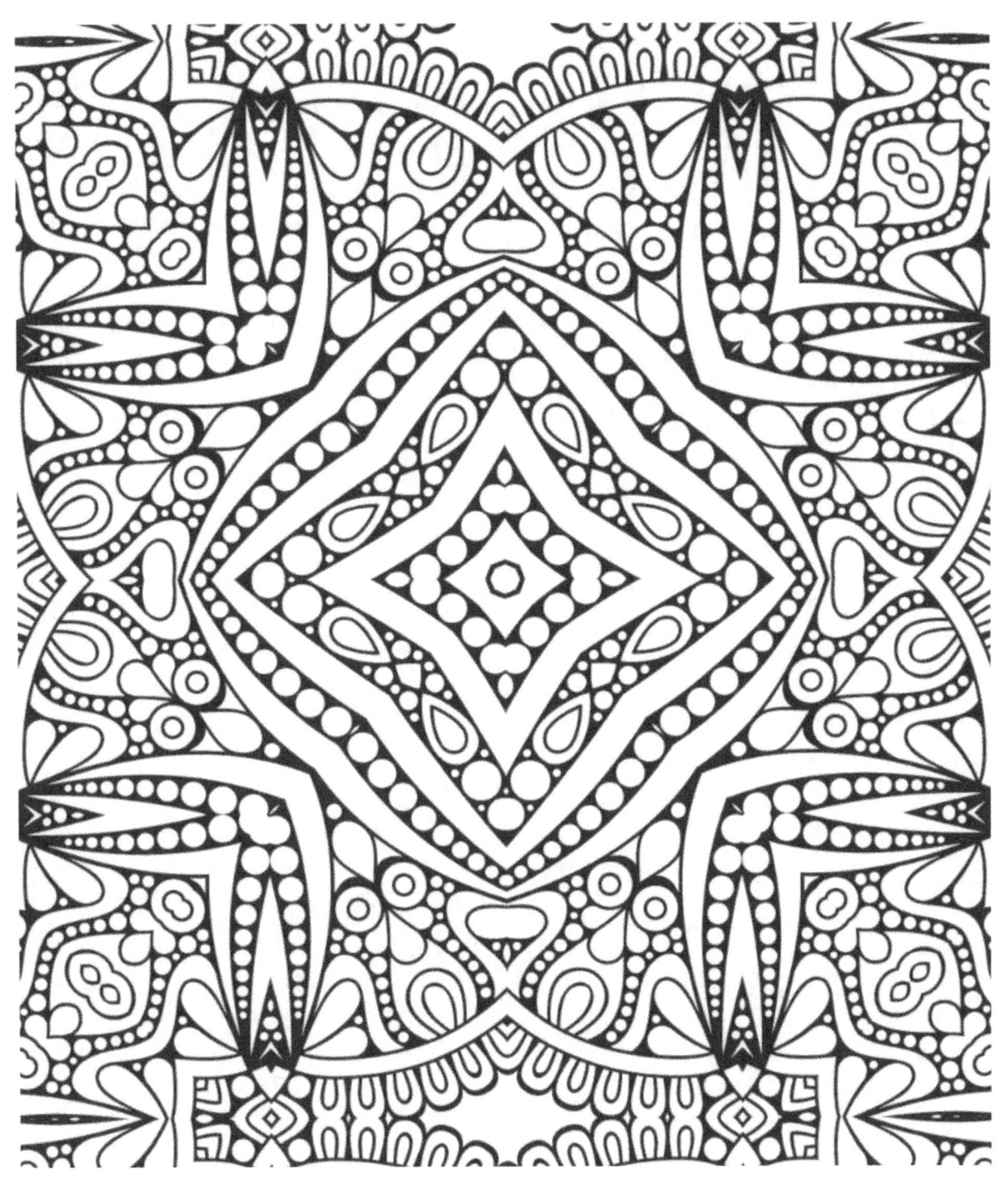

Let your eyes look straight ahead; fix your gaze directly before you.

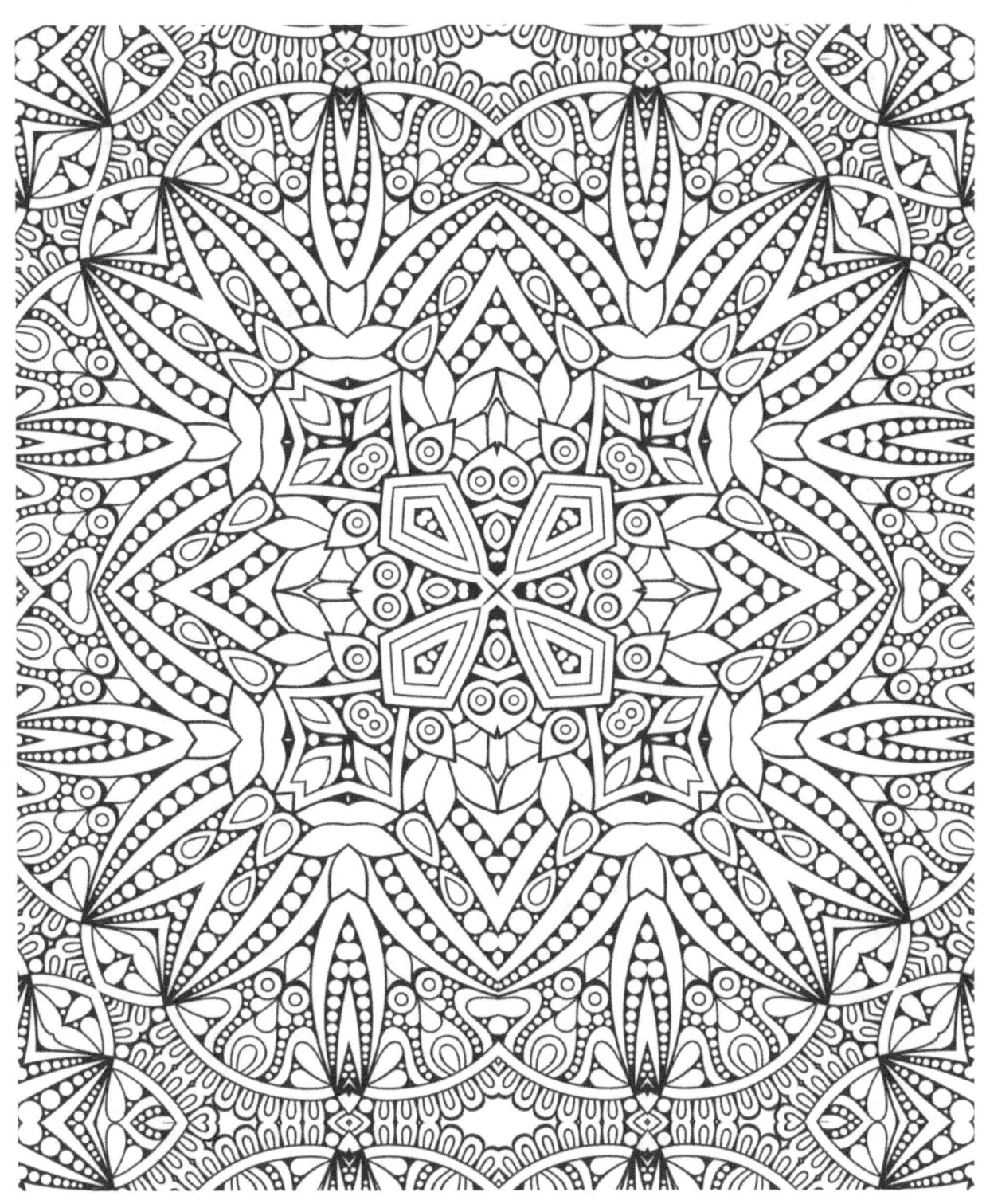

Blessings crown the head of the righteous.

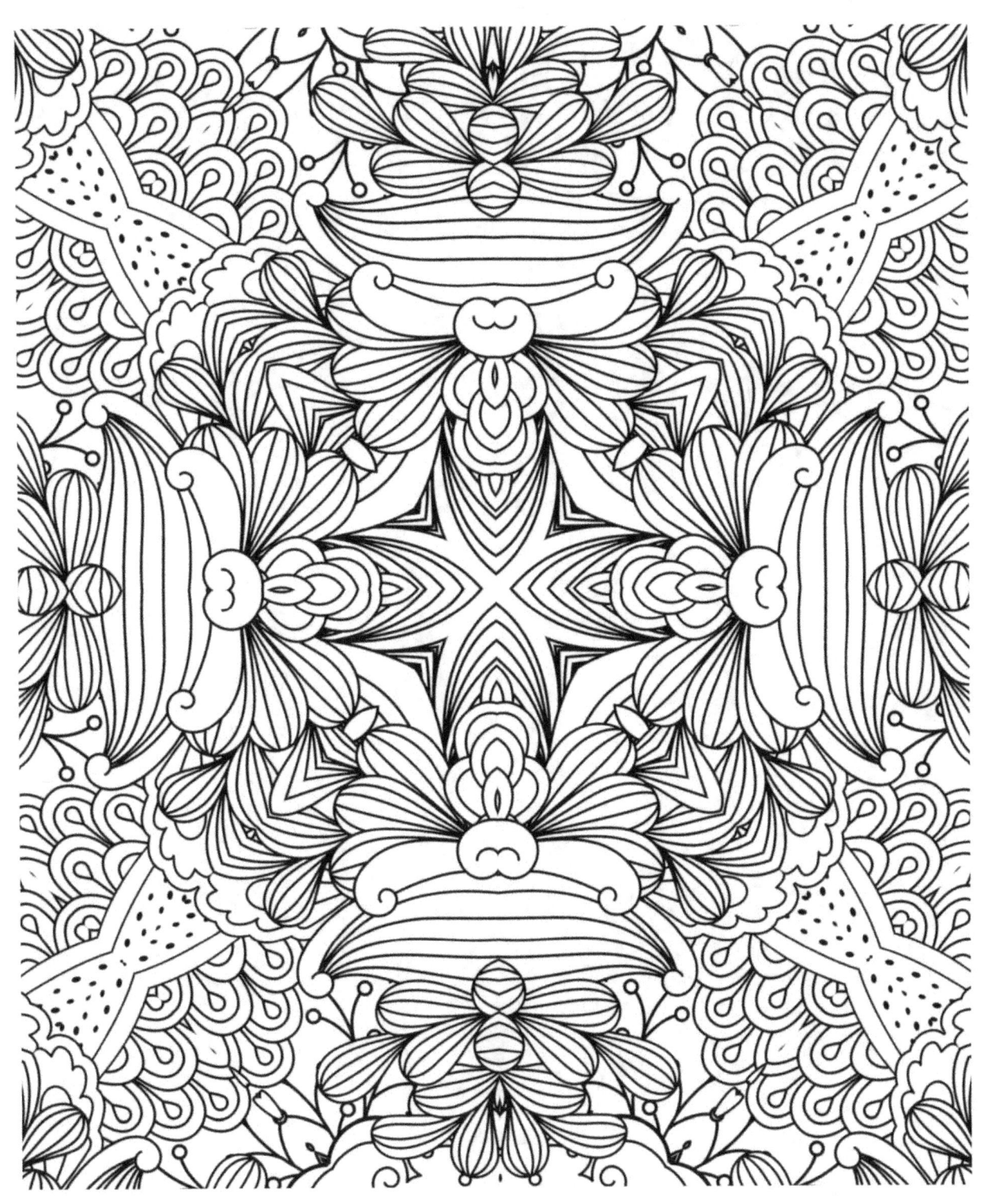

The Lord loves righteousness and justice.

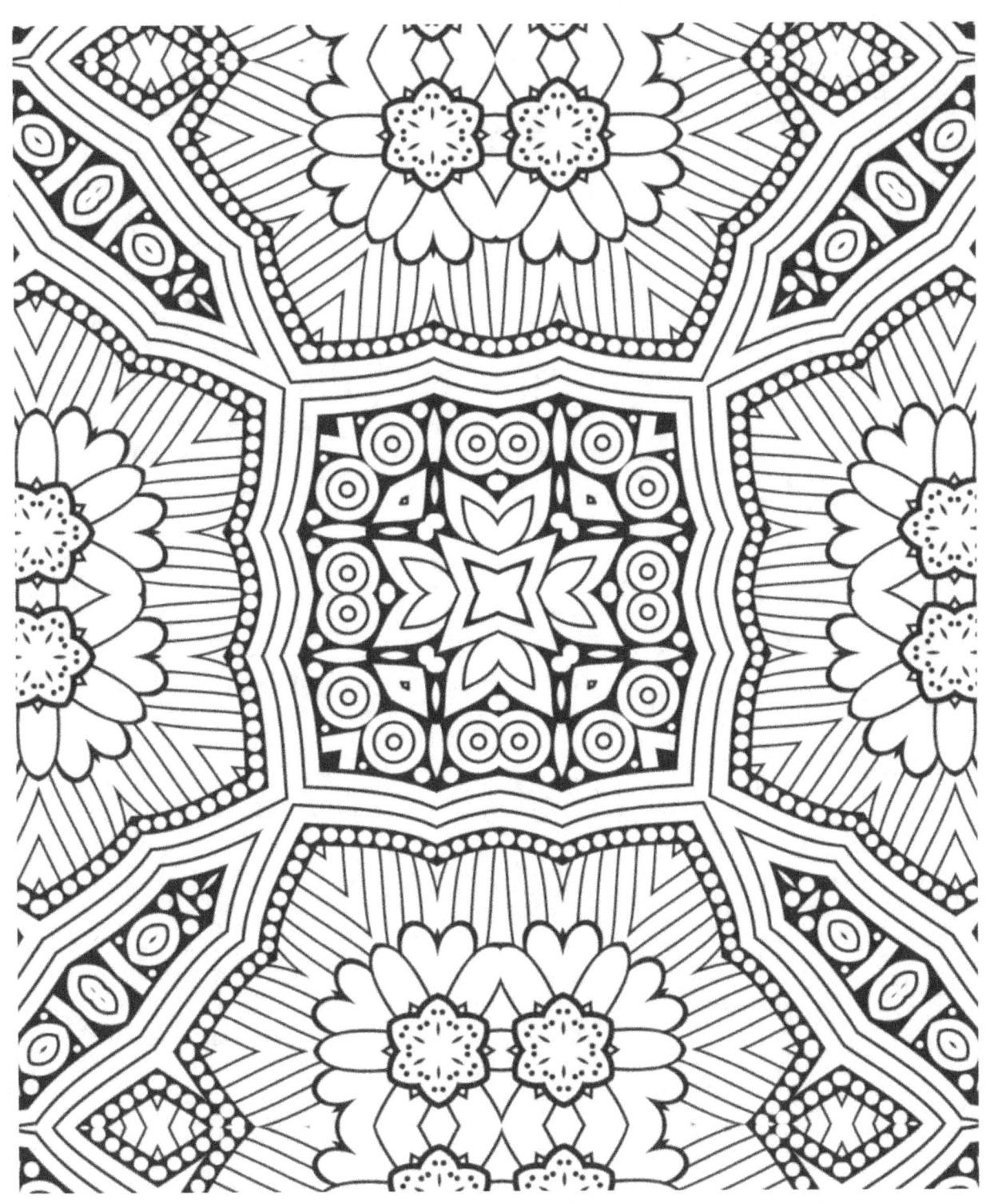

For the eyes of the Lord are on the righteous.

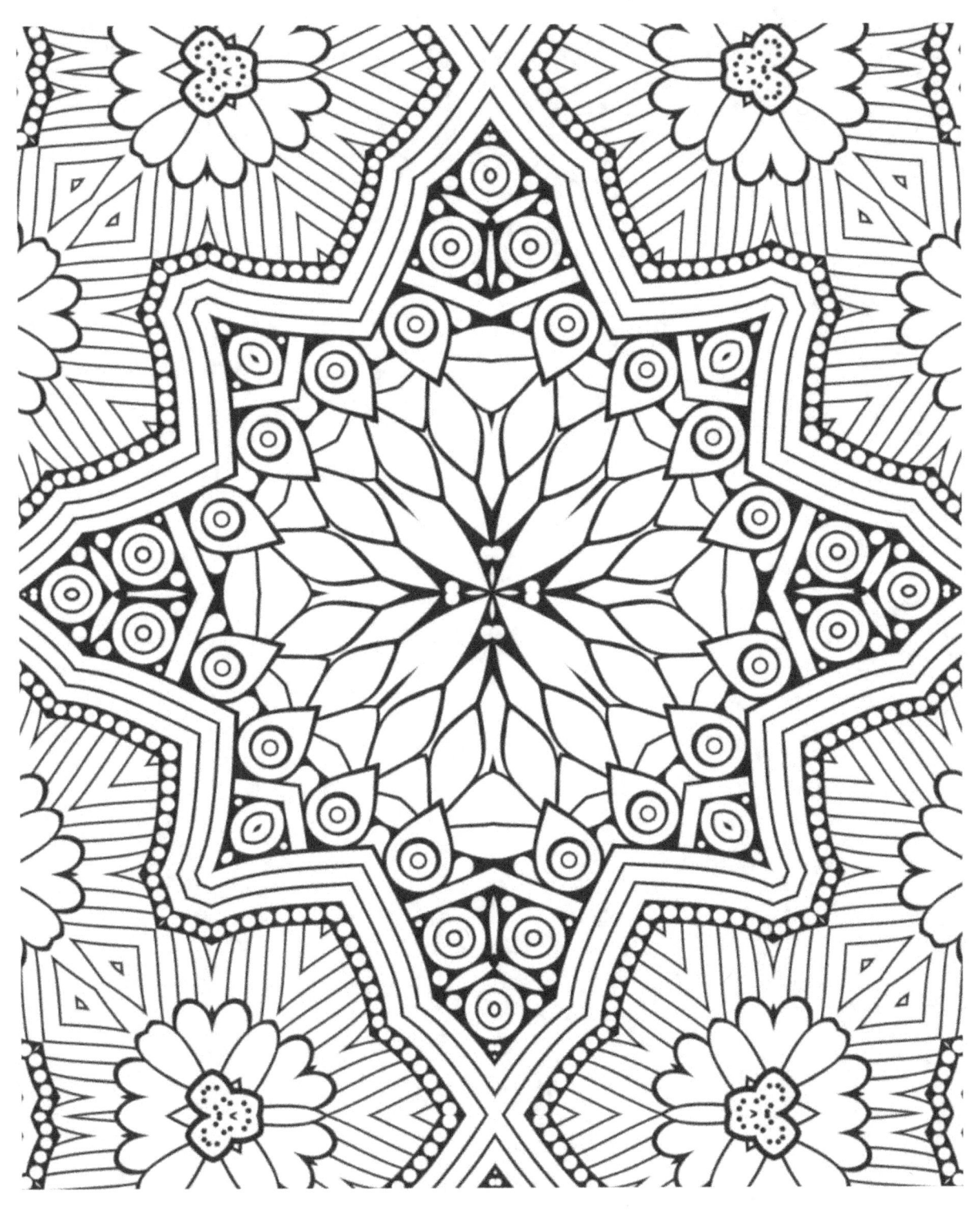

Blessed are those whose ways are blameless.

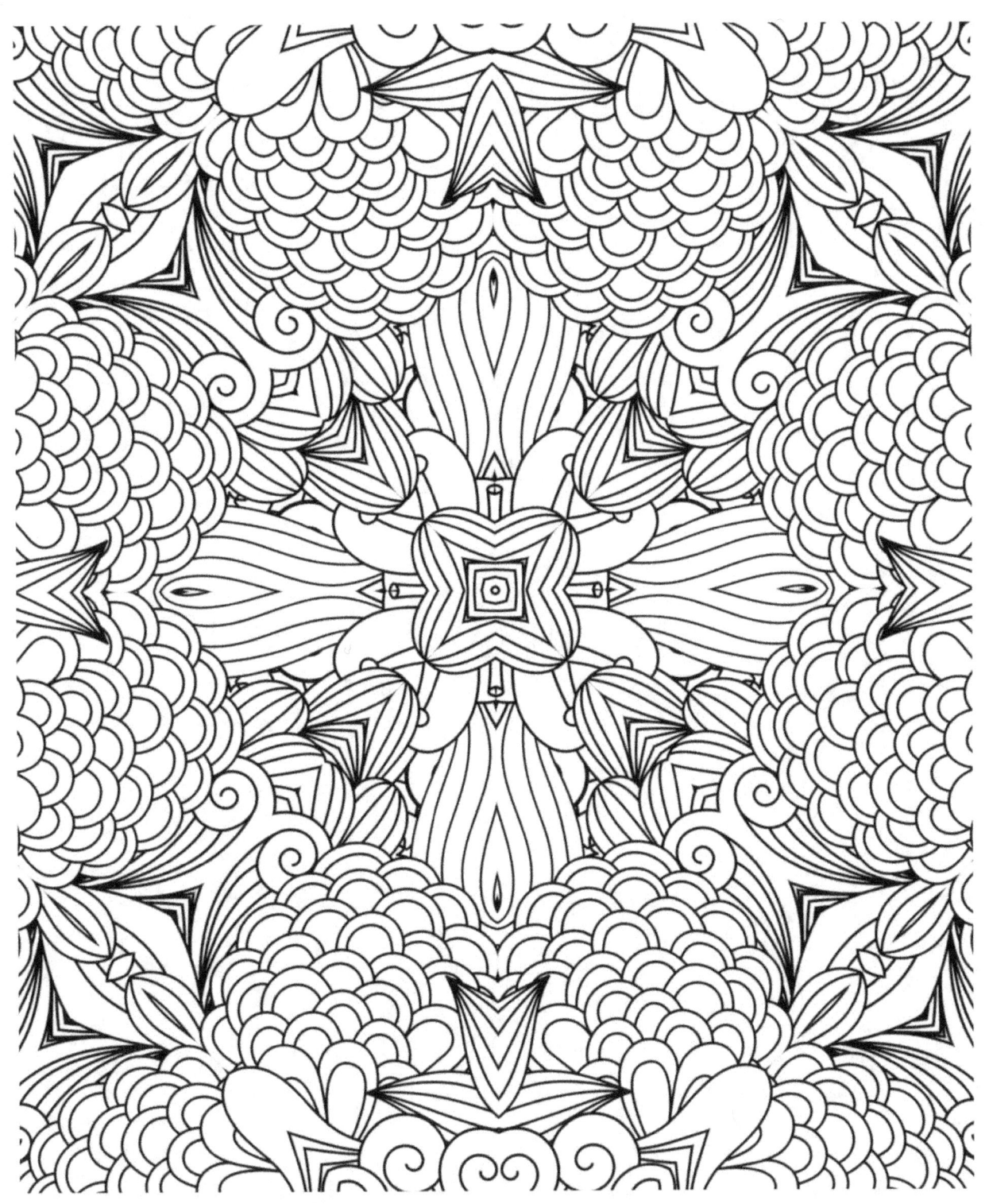

I delight greatly in the Lord; my soul rejoices in my God.

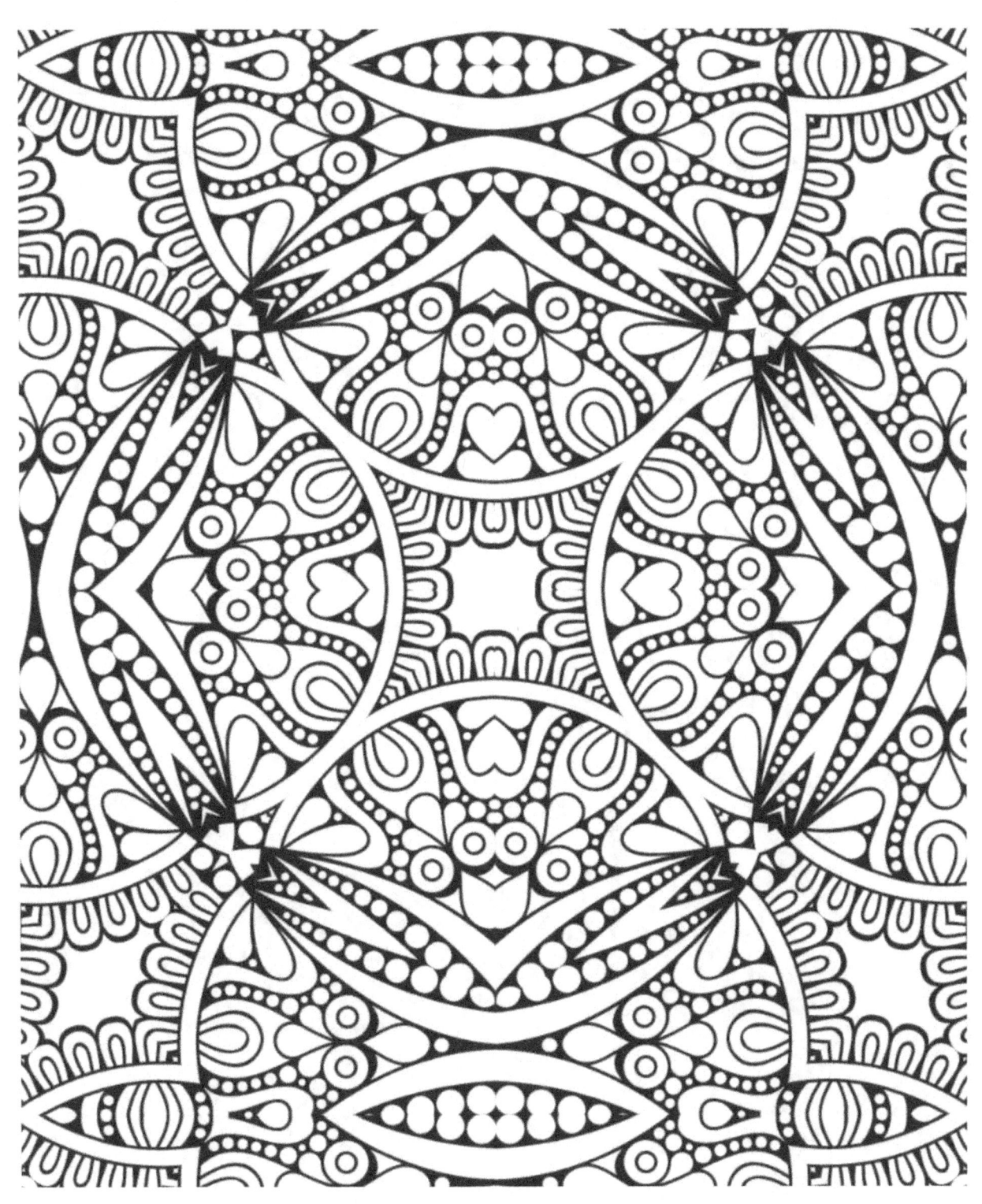

Search me, God, and know my heart.

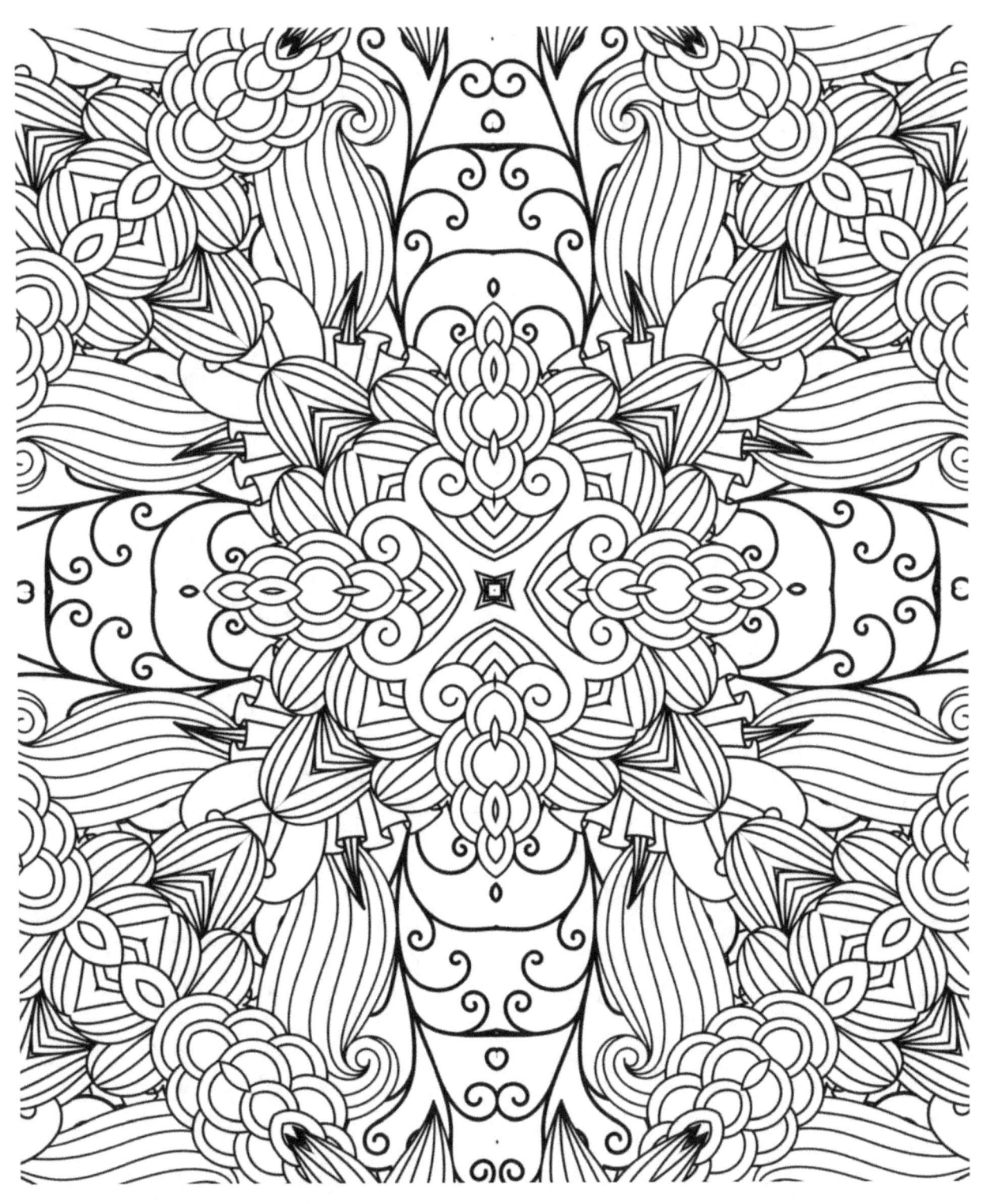

The righteous will live by faith.

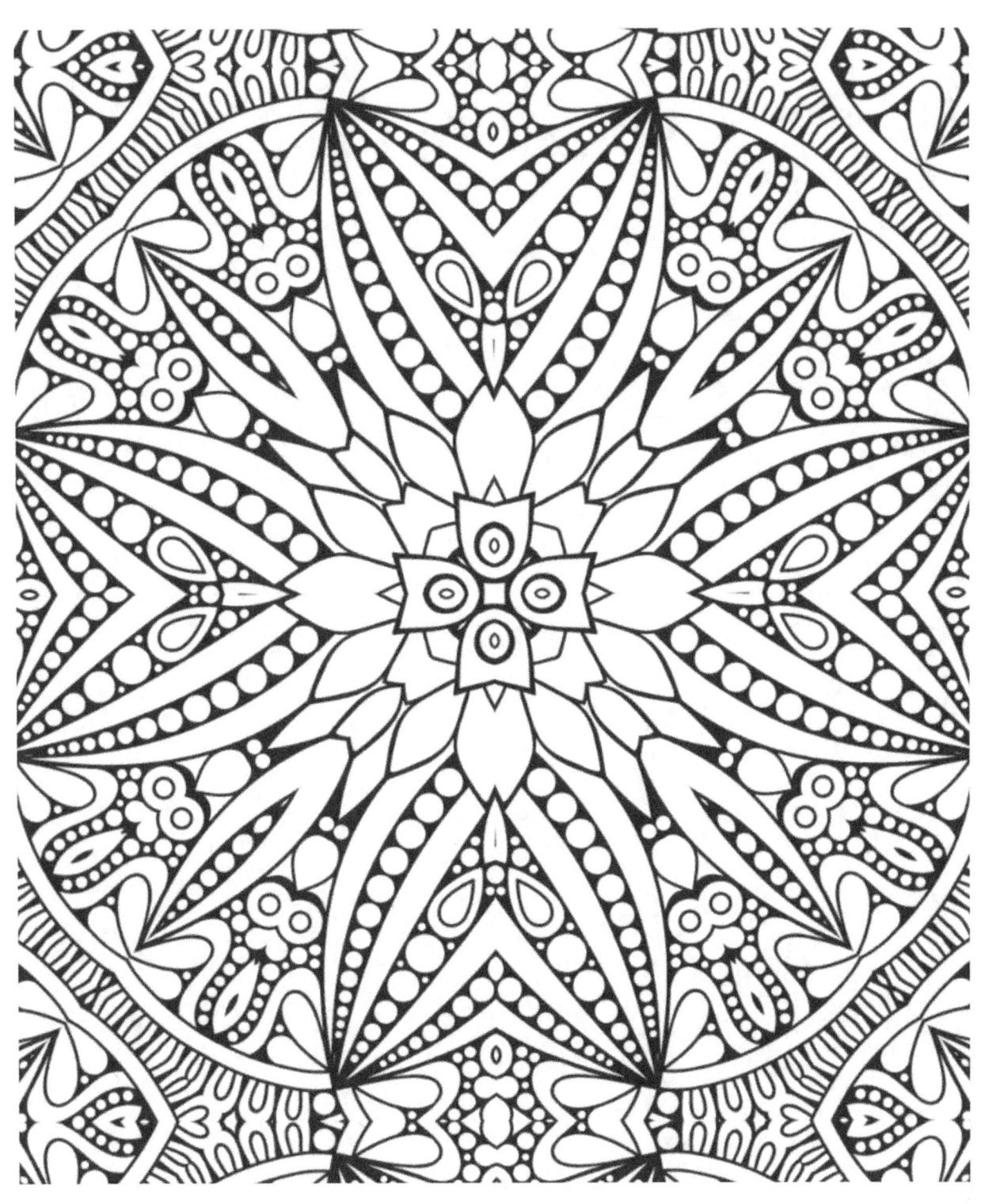

Cast your cares on the Lord, and he will sustain you.

No weapon formed against you shall prosper.

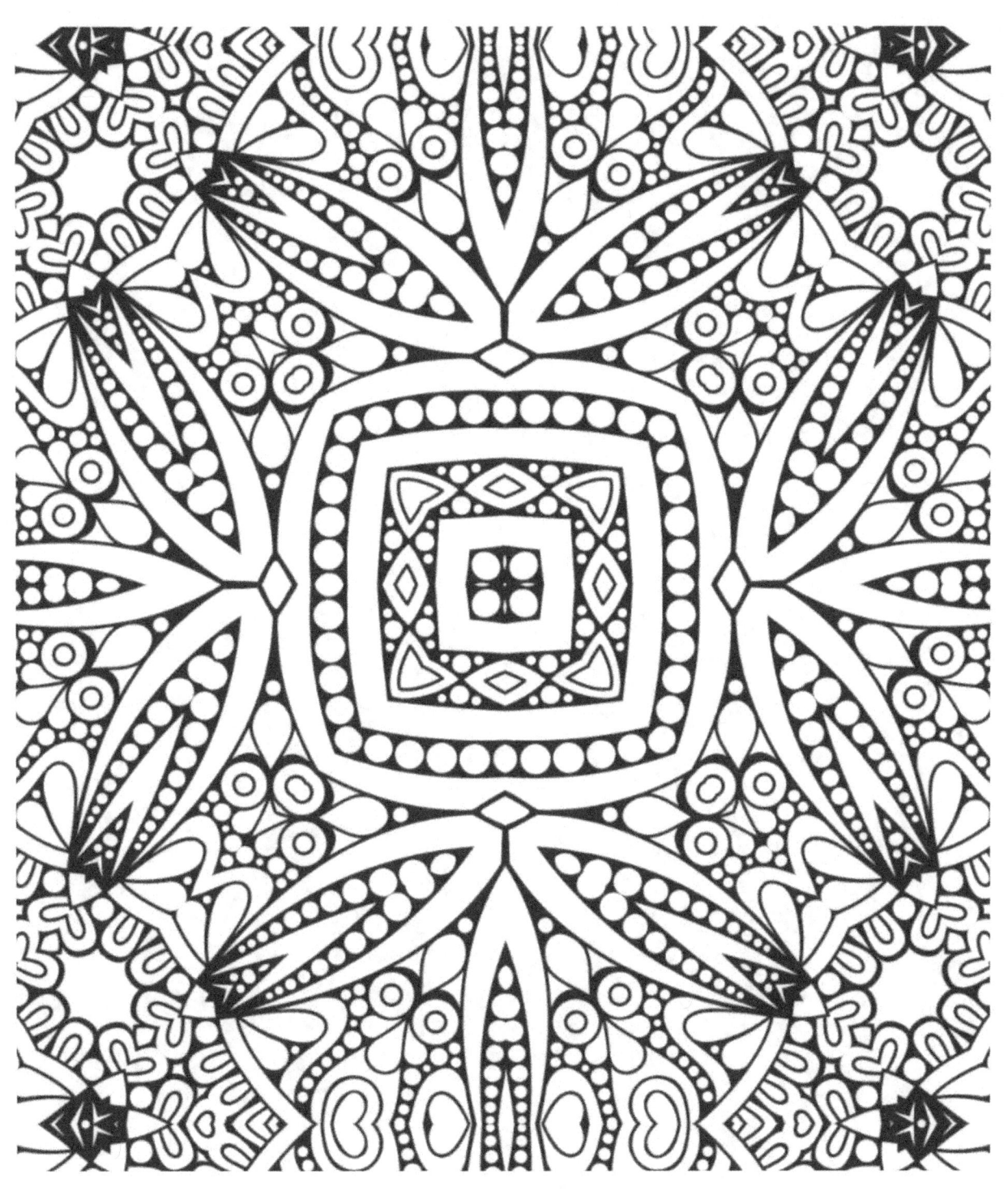

Blessed are those who hunger and thirst for righteousness.

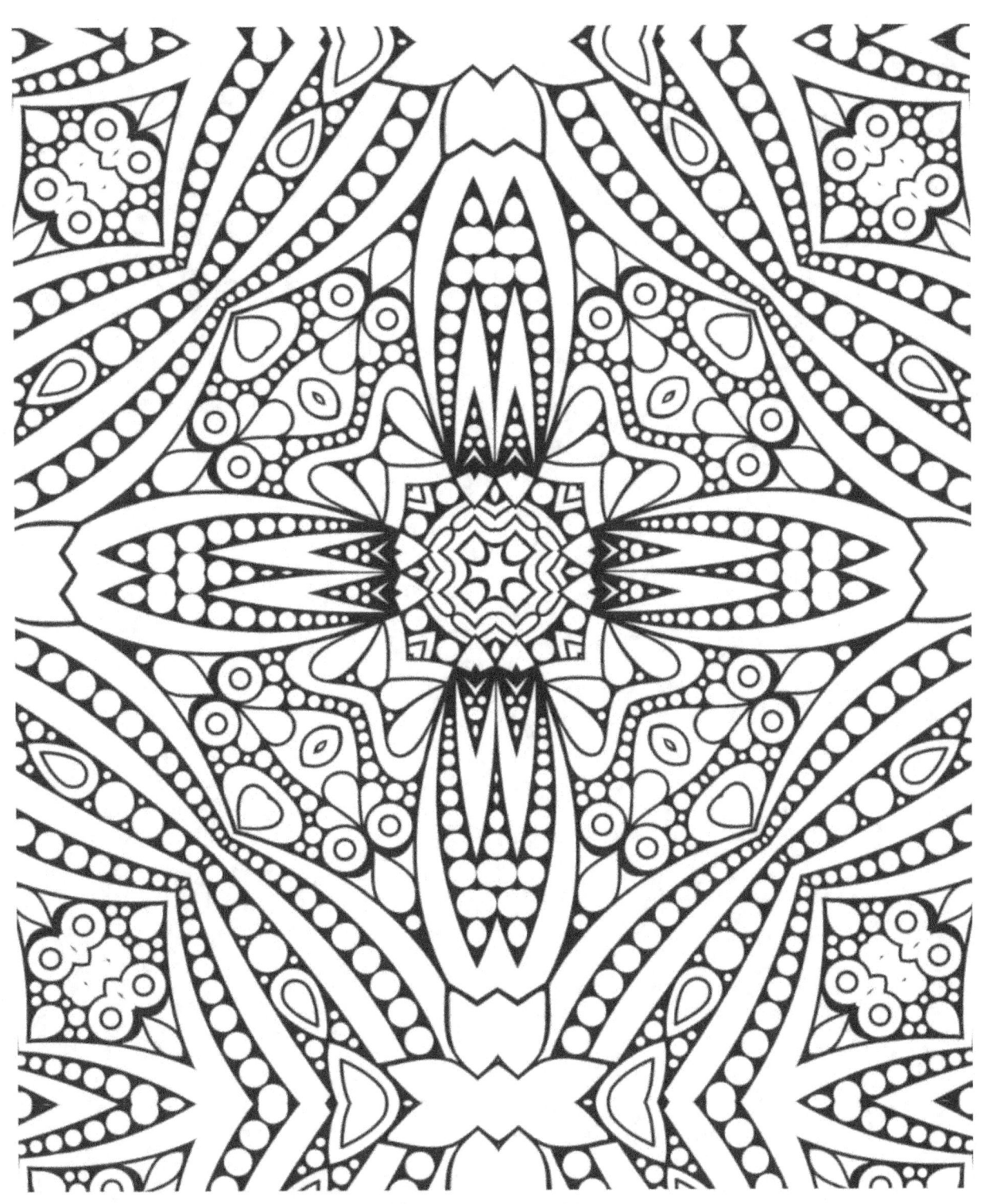

For the Lord loves the just and will not forsake his faithful ones.

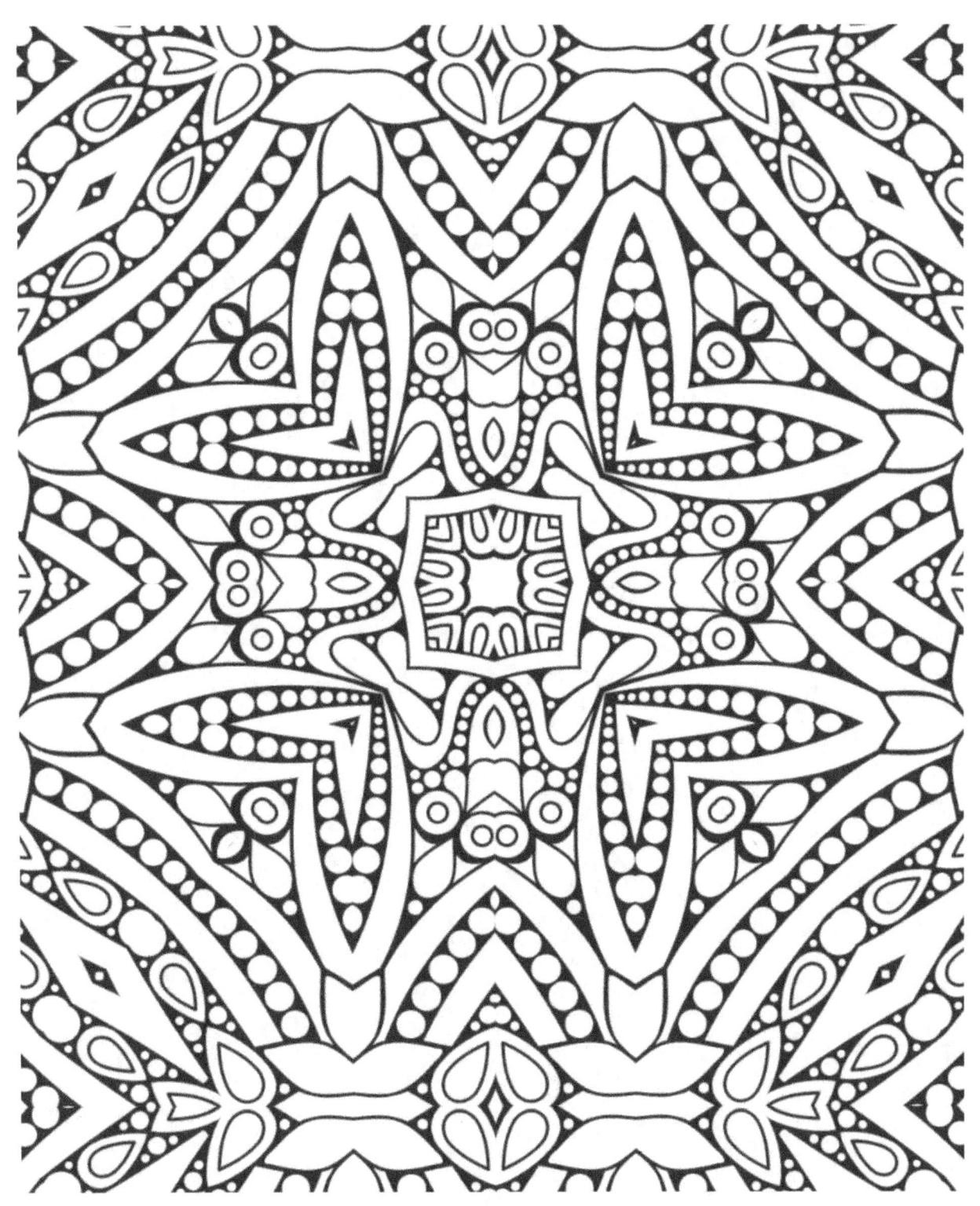

For it is by grace you have been saved, through faith.

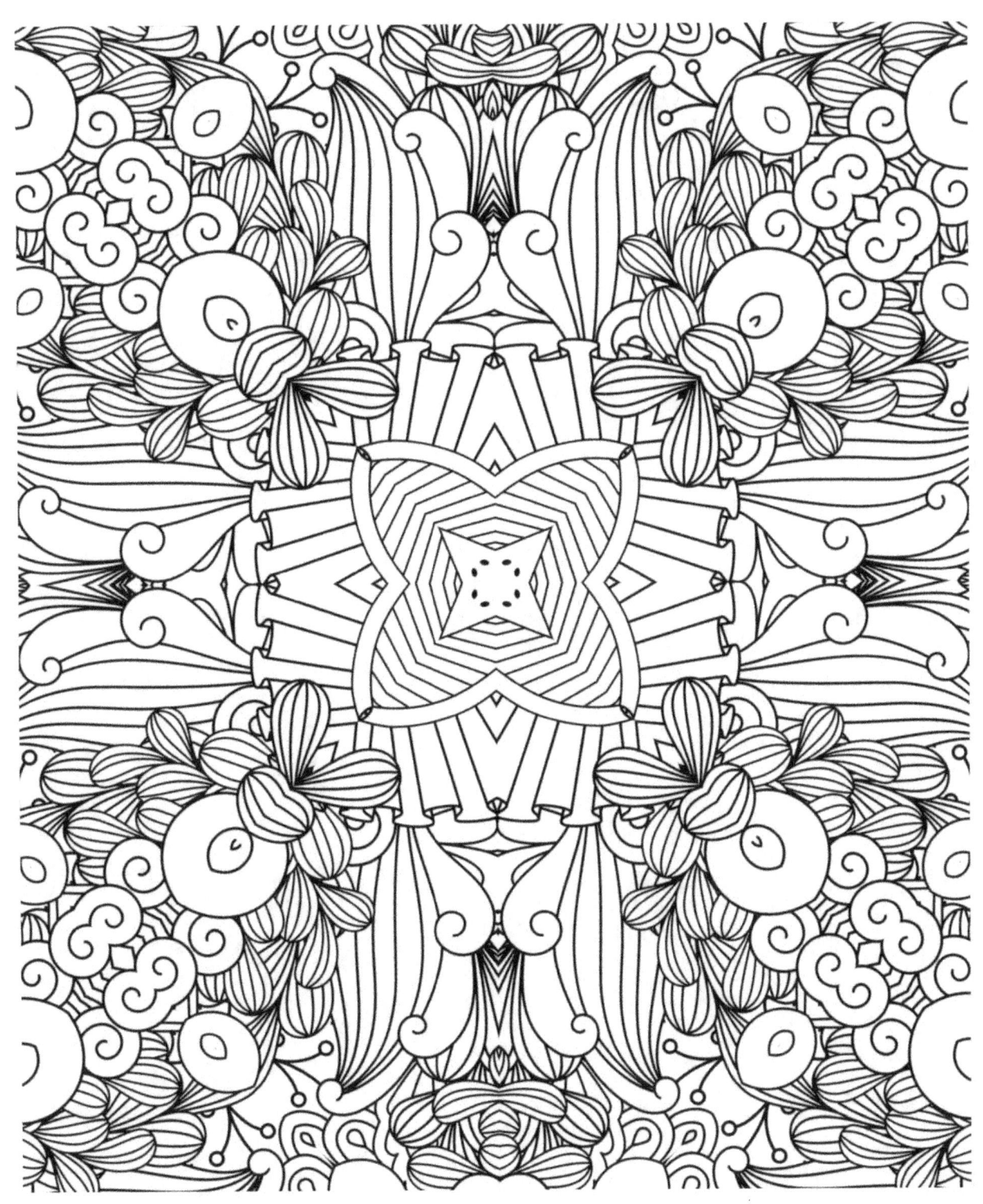

What is impossible with man is possible with God.

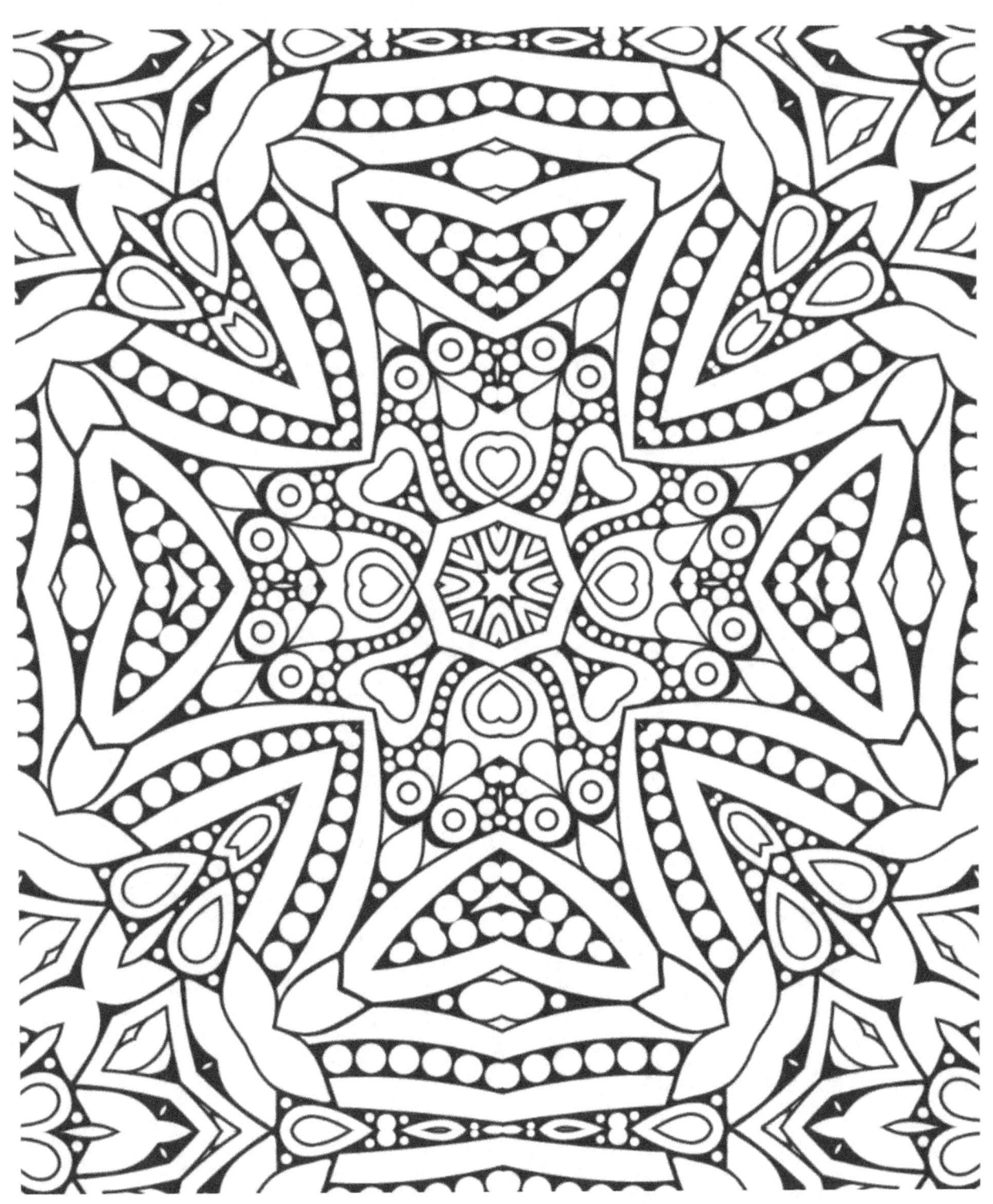

This is the victory that has overcome the world, even our faith.

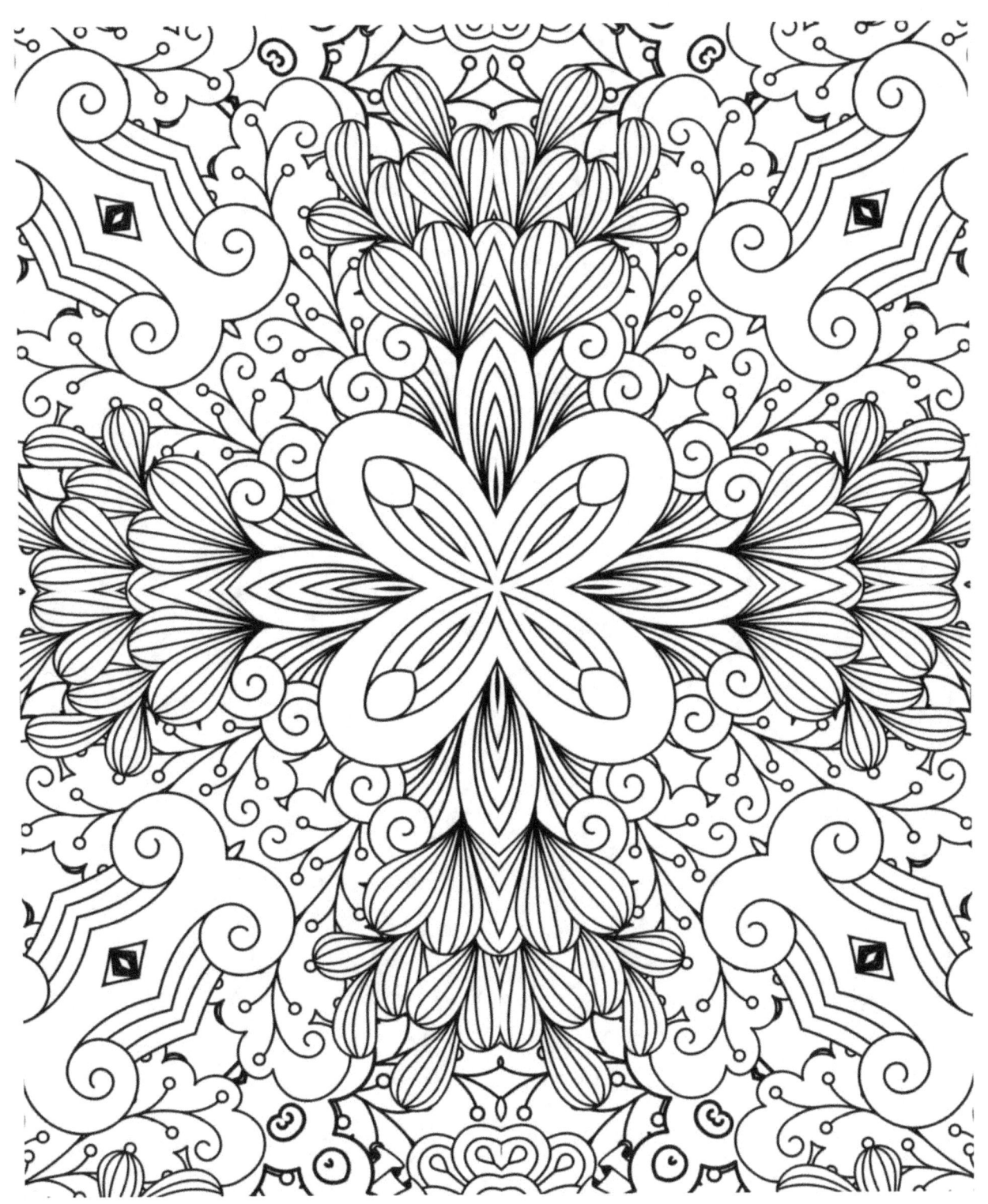

If anyone is in Christ, the new creation has come.

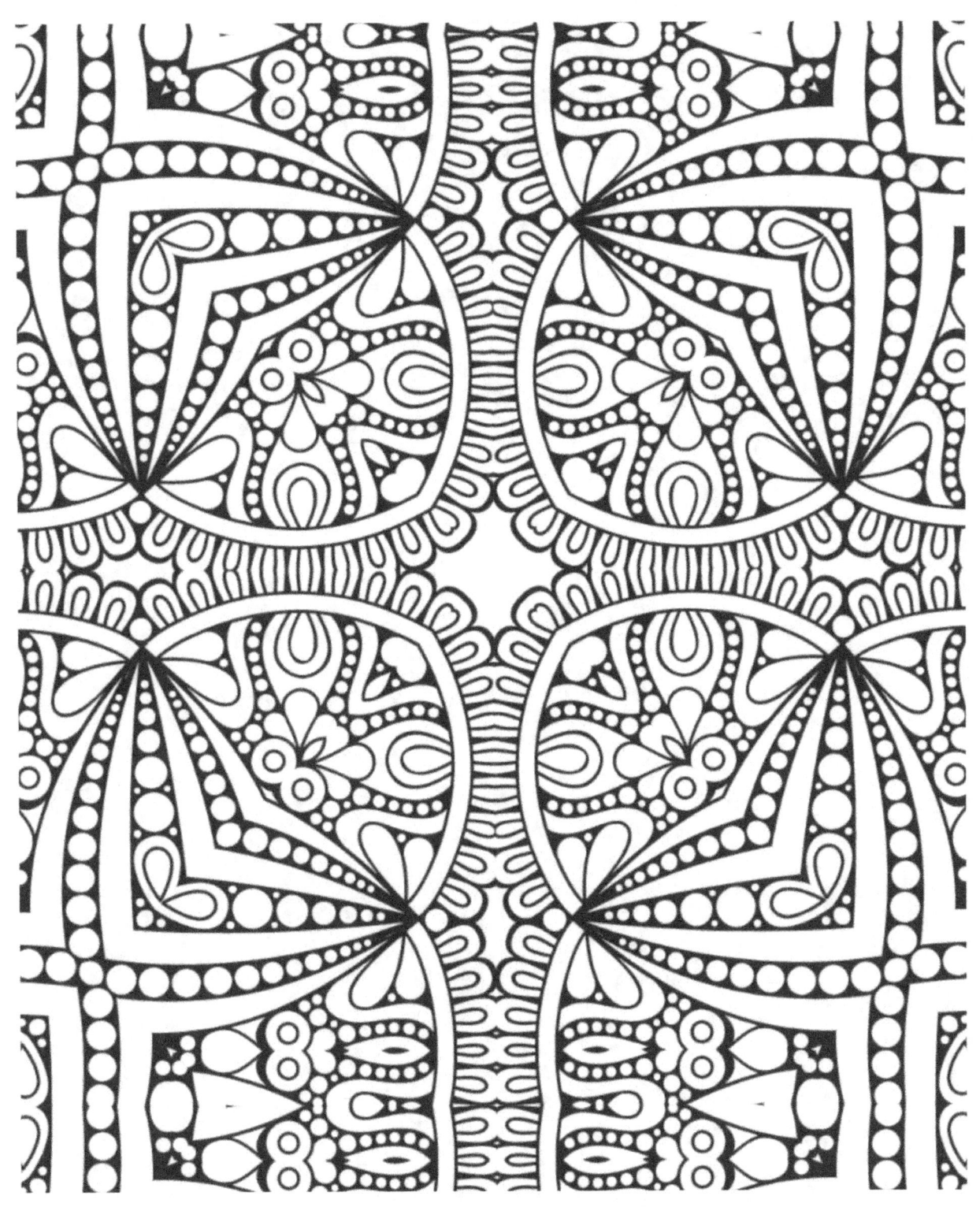

Praise the Lord. Blessed are those who fear the Lord.

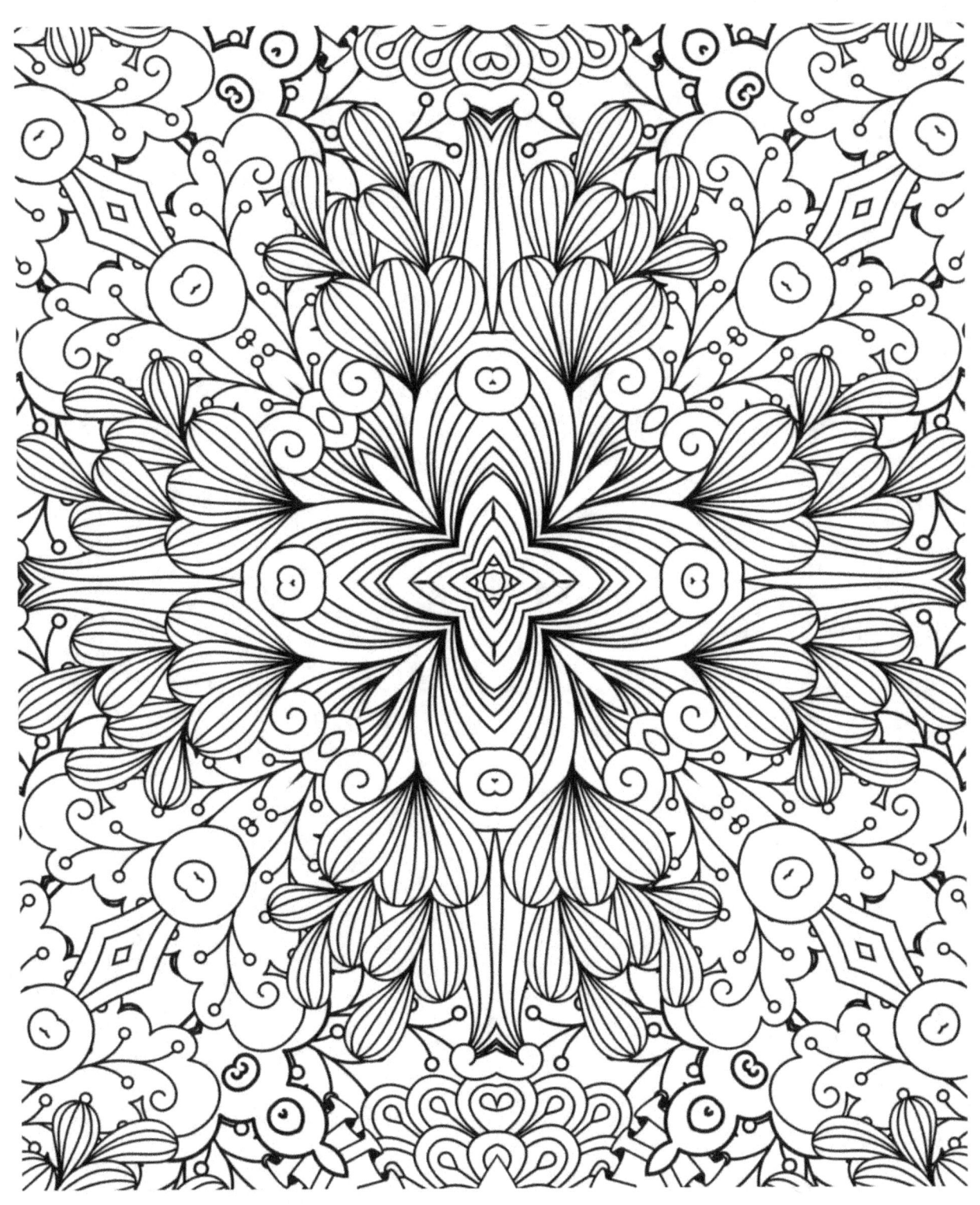

The fear of the Lord is the beginning of knowledge.

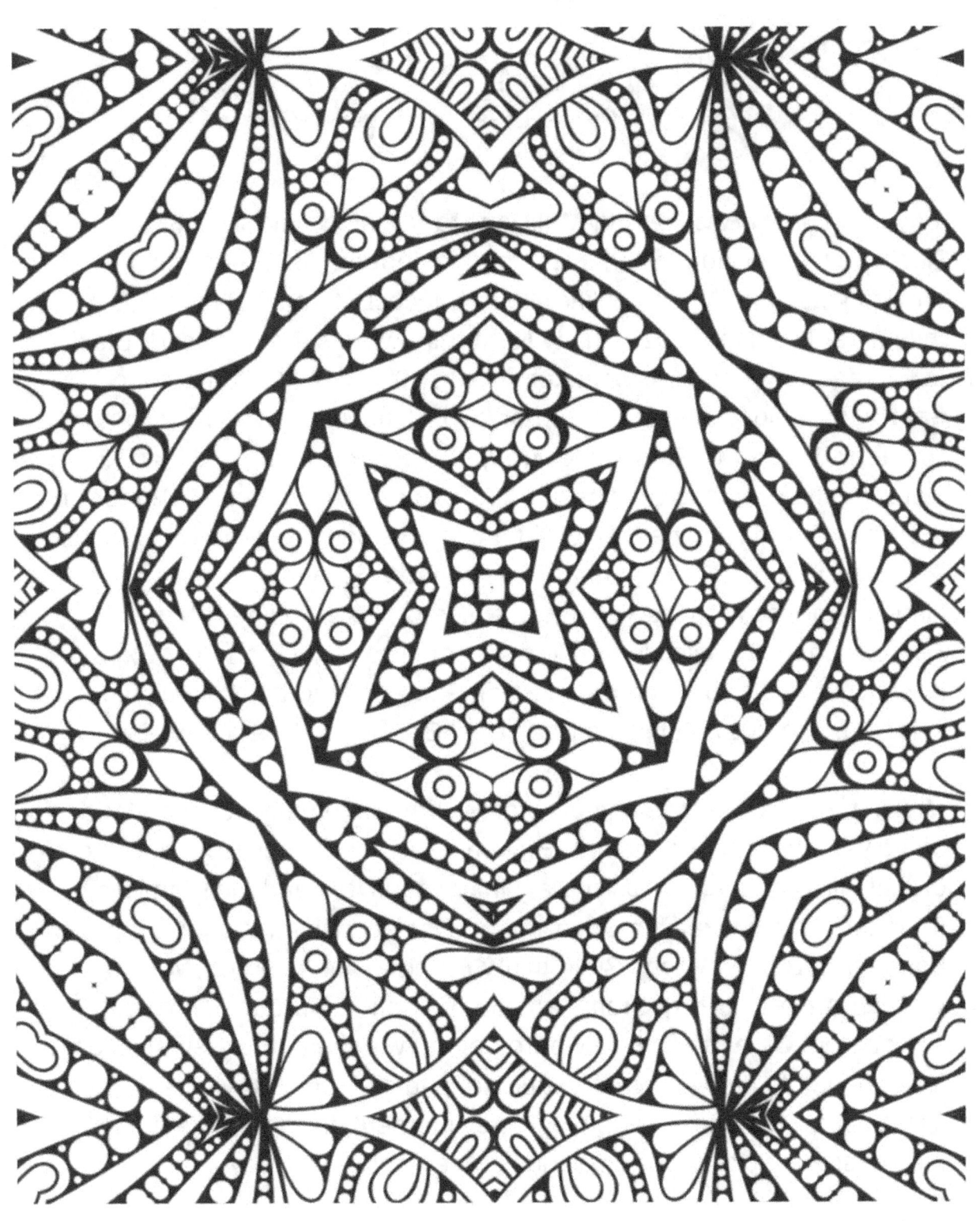

Humility is the fear of the Lord.

About The Author

Twylia Reid is a Best-Selling-Multi-Award-Winning Author and Multi-Published non-fiction writer. Her work has appeared in numerous publications, in print, and online. 2020 Success Women National Top Influencer Nominee, 2019 Trinity Nonprofit Awards Finalist, 2019 Blacks In Government Featured Speaker, 2019 110th NAACP Conference Featured Author/Panelist Moderator, 2019 Unspoken Wounds Women Veteran's Portrait of Personal Courage Award Recipient, 2019 ACHI (Strength In Sisterhood) Magazine Woman of Achievement & Author of the Year Award Nominee, 2018 48th Congressional Legislative Caucus Featured Author, 2019 Winner of The Authors Show Health/Fitness/Wellness Top Female Author, 2018 Winner of The Authors Show Female Non-Fiction Author, The Huffington Post Expert Feature Series "Who's Who –10 Black Female Experts to Watch in 2018" selected, and 2017 American Book Fest Best Book Awards Finalist.

Minister, speaker, entrepreneur, brain-injury-community advocate and caregiver, she's the Founder of Broken Wings, Inc., a 501(c)3 non-profit organization created to assist brain injury survivors and their families, Founder of When Heaven Speaks, LLC book coaching & publishing, Founder of Broken Wings Brain Injury Empowerment Group, Warring Women Arise and Pray Group, and the Executive Producer/Host of the Conquerors Café radio show where her knowledge and expertise is used as a conduit to help empower, educate, and enlighten survivors & caregivers of traumatic events by teaching them how to create the life they desire in spite of the challenges faced after a tragedy.

Her mantra is "Aspiring to Inspire Others!" To learn more, visit her website at www.twyliareid.com.

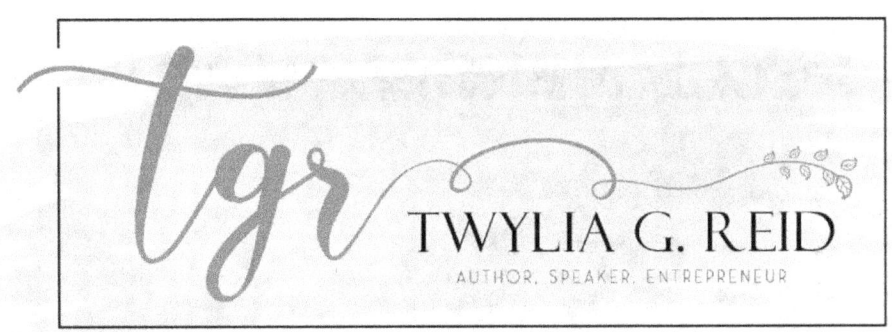

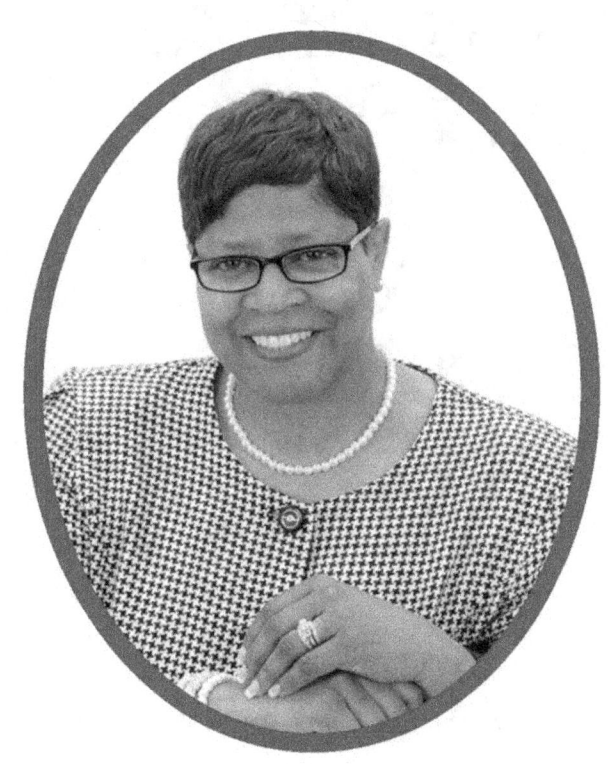

www.TwyliaReid.com
www.whenheavenspeakspublishing.com
www.brokenwingsinc.org

RECOMMENDED READINGS

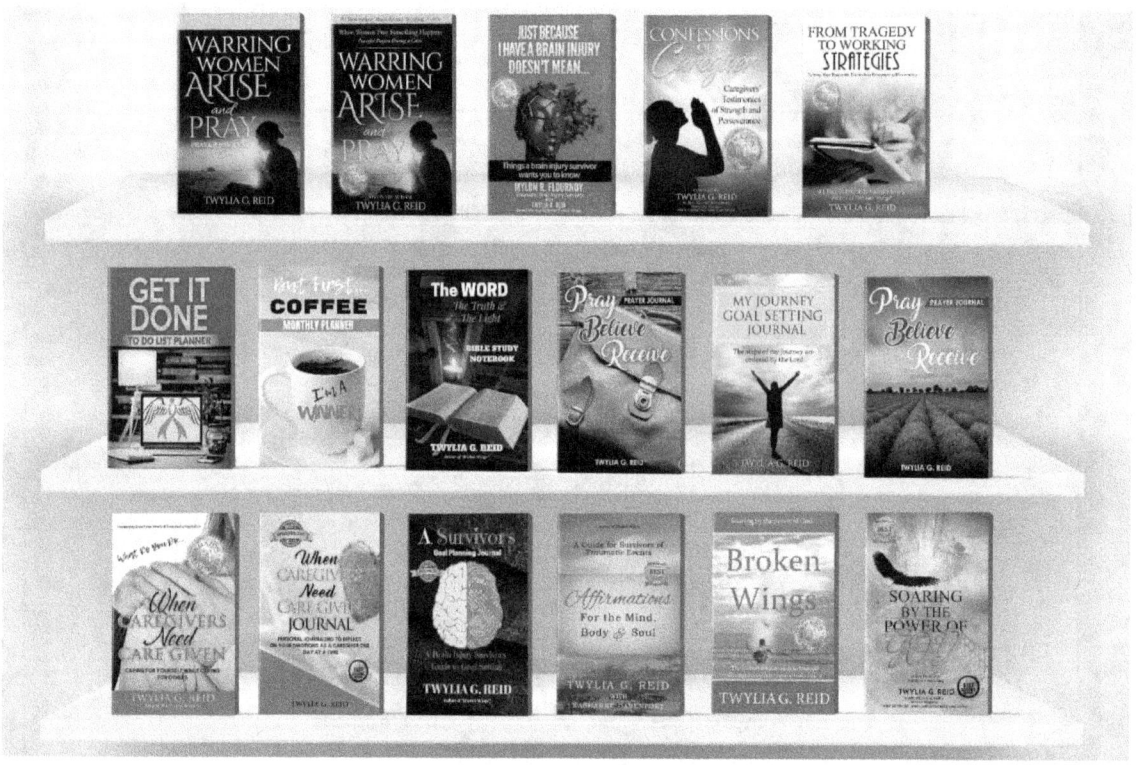

All books can be purchased from my website at
www.TwyliaReid.com
or
www.amazon.com/author/twyliareid

I pray this book is uplifting to your soul as you find peace and tranquility in the images on each page.

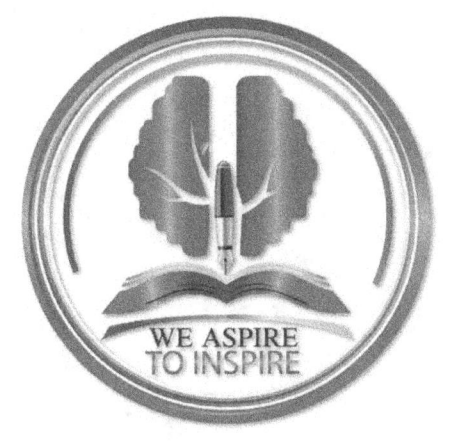

WHEN HEAVEN SPEAKS, LLC

www.whenheavenspeakspublishing.com

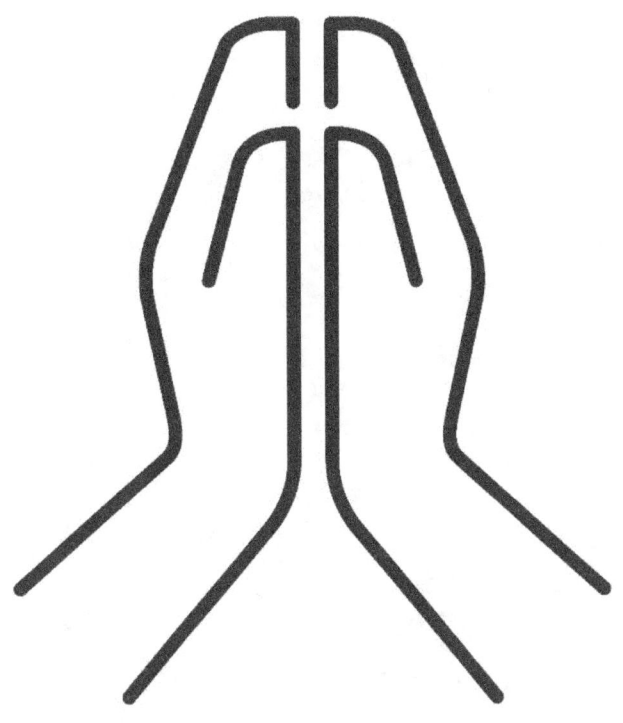